Worldview Witnessing
How to Confidently Share Christ with Anyone

Worldview Witnessing
How to Confidently Share Christ with Anyone

by

Freddy Davis

Copyright ©2007
All rights reserved. Printed in the United States of America.
No part of this publication may be reproduced, stored in a
retrieval system, or transmitted, in any form or by any
means electronic, mechanical, photocopying, recording,
or otherwise, without the prior written permission of the author.

ISBN 1-58961-563-8

Published by PageFree Publishing, Inc.
PO Box 60
Otsego, MI 49078
www.pagefreepublishing.com

What People Are Saying About This Book

Worldview Witnessing presents a good approach to evangelism in this postmodern and highly diverse era. Freddy's personal experience in missions gives him an authentic and credible perspective on cross-cultural evangelism.

> Dr. Tal Davis
> *Strategic Evangelism Coordination*
> *North American Mission Board of the*
>   *Southern Baptist Convention*

Freddy Davis' book brings to the discussion of evangelism the reality of the need to be both culturally sensitive and relevant concerning the presentation of the Good News of Jesus Christ. This book helps Christians see the importance of understanding the receivers of the Gospel and their points of view. The book provides an understanding of where others are theologically and how to speak into their experience in a contextualized way. A must read for anyone, but especially those of the emergent culture trying to reach post-moderns.

> Dr. Jeffrey Johnson
> *Director of Evangelism*
> *American Baptist Churches USA*

As the pastor of a local church I believe that this book should be in the hands of every church member. It provides valuable insight into the heart of God concerning his desire and expectation that we share our faith with others. It is evident to me that most believers feel inadequate to share their faith and Christian experience with others, even those whom they know well. With this book, we can soon be on our way to touching our world in a tremendous way for Jesus Christ.

> Pastor Larry Millender
> *Abundant Life Fellowship World Outreach Center*
> *Tallahassee, Florida*

"An outstanding textbook on making yourself be intentional. Freddy has us get into the world of an unbeliever with understanding, with respect, with care and with support. All this culminates to build an effective witness for Christ".

> Pastor Kent Nottingham
> *Calvary Chapel, Tallahassee*

Table of Contents

Introduction 1

Part I - Prepping for Witness 5
   Chapter 1 - What Do You Believe? 7
   Chapter 2 - How Are Various Belief
   Systems Different? 19
   Chapter 3 - Your Understanding of God Determines
   Your Effectiveness 33
   Chapter 4 - Your Understanding of People Determines
   Your Effectiveness 43

Part II - How to Witness to a Non-Christian
Based on Worldview 51
   Chapter 5 - Think Like a Missionary 53
   Chapter 6 - Think Relationship First 61
   Chapter 7 - Elicit Their Beliefs - Ask the 7
   Worldview Questions 67
   Chapter 8 - Create a Respectful Atmosphere 73
   Chapter 9 - Be Ready When an Opportunity Presents
   Itself 81
   Chapter 10 - Speak with Boldness 91
   Chapter 11 - Don't Try to Win Points 97
   Chapter 12 - Think Long Term 103
   Chapter 13 - Relationship Road 111

Introduction

I almost hesitated to write a book with the word "witnessing" in the title. It is such a loaded word. Some people think of having to memorize a heavy duty canned speech. Others think of having to make cold calls to strangers and ask them about one of the most private parts of their lives. The image of some is of having to initiate an uncomfortable confrontation.

I grew up having the opportunity to experience all of those things. When I became a Christian as a mid teen, it was a powerfully moving experience and I jumped into my new Christian life with both feet. I learned how to "witness" and took many opportunities to do it. For me, witnessing was defined as, "Sharing the gospel of Jesus Christ with lost people and leaving the results up to God." This is certainly not a bad definition, but over the years I have learned that there are broader implications than what may appear on the surface.

The methodologies I learned almost always involved finding a person who would listen to me, whipping out my Bible, the Four Spiritual Laws, or some other witnessing tool, and running through the plan of salvation. At the end I would bring the person to a point of decision. If they accepted Christ and "prayed the prayer," I rejoiced and went on my way. If they didn't say "no," but were not yet ready to make the step, I encouraged them and went on my way. If they said "no," I said goodbye and went on my way.

In virtually every case, especially in cold call situations, witnessing was an event that happened at a point in time and ended. If it ended well, there was at least a chance that they would find a church to get involved with. If it ended badly, I would probably never see them again. In any case, it rarely ended in any kind of a continuing relationship where I could keep check on them over a period of time.

It is not that "event" witnessing is a bad thing. But statistics show that the huge majority of people who ultimately come to know Christ, do so as the result of a relationship with someone – not from a chance cold call encounter. The only problem is, purposeful relationships are hard.

This is not to say that all relationships are hard. There are certain ones that we engage as an ongoing part of our life routine. What is hard is to intentionally make and use relationships as a means of witness. Not only do we have to learn the mechanics of how to present the gospel message, we also have to live our lives before people in a way that backs up what we are saying.

When we look at the big picture, the process is what it is. We do need to learn how to make a gospel presentation so that we can introduce people to Christ when we have the opportunity. But this book seeks to change the paradigm somewhat. I no longer look at a witnessing opportunity simply as an event. It is very rare for me to enter a cold call situation and just start sharing the plan of salvation. I can do it if I need to, and there are occasions when that happens. But I have dramatically changed my perspective. Rather than just spouting off with the message, I now want to engage people in a way that gives me the best possibility to impact their lives. That will rarely happen in a cold call situation where I and the one I am talking with are both uncomfortable.

There is a better way. Yes, it requires learning how to share the gospel. You can't get away from the need to have a basic foundation of knowledge, and a method to deliver it.

But it requires even more. It requires a person to get a grasp of worldview. You can't legitimately get into the most personal parts of another person's life unless you truly understand where they are coming from. An understanding of worldview helps you get there. Understanding worldview also gives you a powerful foundation for understanding your own faith. You can never have total confidence about sharing your faith if you are not completely convinced that it is the truth. And this book is all about having that kind of confidence.

But it requires one thing more. It requires that you be willing to engage people in an actual relationship, and use that relationship as a tool for sharing the gospel.

Right off the bat, all of this may seem a bit daunting for some. Who has the time for all of that? And you may be right. This might not be for everyone. It is, actually, only for:

- those who believe that God is a real person who wants every human being to know him personally,
- those who believe that God wants every Christian to be an instrument to make that introduction,
- those who are tired of being afraid and frustrated about their own personal witness, and
- those who want to become excited about their own spiritual journey.

If you don't care about these things, this book is not for you. But if you do care, this could be the beginning of an entirely new chapter of your spiritual journey, and your effectiveness in living the Christian life.

Part I
Prepping for Witness

On occasion, I have had the opportunity to share my faith with someone who has tried to dismiss my Christian faith, and to witness to me about their beliefs. This happened not long back when a person I met (I will call him Tom) tried to introduce me to Enlightened Theism (ET) – a new religion he and a friend were starting. He actually had a series of statements written out describing the doctrines of the faith. It was somewhat disorganized, but contained most of the components of a faith system – a doctrine of God, of man and of salvation.

As he tried to proselytize me, I did not want to lose the opportunity to share my faith with him, as well. In order to do that, there were two things I needed to know. First, I had to learn the doctrines of his belief system so I would know where he was coming from. It would be senseless to engage him in a way that didn't make sense to his way of thinking. Secondly, I had to know my own beliefs about God, man and salvation. How could I share what I didn't know? But I have acquired knowledge of these two things, and it allowed me to share a very comprehensive witness with him.

Chapter 1
What Do You Believe?

I am a fairly big sports fan. I particularly enjoy football and baseball. I also participate in karate and play a little tennis with my son (though I am not very good at that). I am not a huge basketball or hockey fan, though I do enjoy watching it sometimes, especially during playoff season when you really do have the very best teams going up against one another. But even if I am not a big fan of a particular sport, I do greatly admire the athleticism of those who are the very best in their fields.

Because I enjoy sports, I sometimes get into deep conversations with my friends about what is going on in the world of sports. But the conversations vary according to what sport we are talking about. I know a pretty good bit about football and baseball, so my conversations can be fairly detailed when I talk about those topics. I can do fairly well with basketball too, though I can't talk about the details of strategy as well as I can with the sports I know more about.

Now, one game I don't really know anything about is cricket. It seems that it is a very popular game in England and throughout the British Commonwealth. When we lived overseas in Eastern Europe, the only English language radio station on the air was the British Broadcasting Corporation (BBC). It was great for world news, but the sporting news focused mostly on sports of interest to Britons. Whenever a big international cricket meet was going on, we always got a full rundown on all of the cricket news. They would talk about the wickets, bails and stumps and how many runs were scored, the performance of the bowler, how many overs they played and on and on. As they talked about the game, I had no idea what they were talking about - and still don't. That sport is of no interest to me and I don't know its rules or strategy. If I wanted to tell someone about the game, I wouldn't even know where to begin.

It is not an overstatement to assert that a person is not able to teach or share what they do not know. This is certainly true in sports, and it is true as it relates to sharing the gospel, as well. If we have any interest in sharing the gospel with other people, we are going to have to learn the basics.

I feel fairly confident, though, that a lack of knowledge is not the biggest reason why so few are willing to share their faith. I think that distinction may go to the state of a person's heart and personal morality. But even if it is not the most common reason, lack of knowledge is certainly the most fundamental.

Generally you will find a small hand full of people in most churches who are capable of walking a person step by step through the process of becoming a believer. But compare that with the total number of people in the congregation, and typically it will be a very small percentage. The ones who tend to do it are normally a very small core of the most faithful in the church.

Now there are certainly many reasons why so few Christians are willing to share their faith. People use such excuses as, "I don't know how," "nobody ever taught me how," "it is too hard," "I don't like confronting people," and so on. But every excuse is nothing more than a shallow pretext. The fact is, Christ himself told his followers that it is a part of our Christian responsibility to share the gospel. This does not mean that we

WHAT DO YOU BELIEVE?

have to run around and aggressively confront everybody we come into contact with. It does mean that we need to know how to do it when the opportunity presents itself.

As a pastor, there have been numerous times when I have had people come up to me and tell me about a friend of theirs that I needed to talk to in order to share the gospel. Now don't get me wrong. I am always more than happy to do it. And in those situations, I was glad that they cared enough about their friends to bring them to me. But the truth is, they should have been able to do it themselves.

But even more basic than being able to specifically walk through a gospel presentation, I believe that most Christians have a terrible lack of even a basic understanding of the foundational Christian beliefs. Many couldn't even give a simple list of what those most basic beliefs are.

So just what are the most fundamental beliefs of the Christian faith? There are, of course, some other issues that will need to be addressed as we move forward, but we cannot even start the process until we deal with the "basic belief" issue. Effective witness requires a foundational knowledge of your own beliefs. But you don't have to have a PhD in systematic theology to do this. God designed the gospel in a way that makes it possible for every individual to understand and share it.

Obviously the more you know, in any area of life, the more confident and effective you will become. When it comes to our faith in Christ, there is a very simple core of three doctrines that form the basis for a witness. To be effective in sharing your faith, you particularly need to understand the doctrines of God, man and salvation. With a basic knowledge of these three, you will have a foundation upon which to build personal confidence in your own faith, and for explaining to another how they can enter a personal relationship with God.

As we move forward, it must be acknowledged that the

only way we, as Christians, are able to know anything about God is through his revelation of himself to humankind. God is so far beyond our knowing that unless he lets us know of his existence and his character, we simply could not know anything about him. This revelation comes in three different forms, his creation (nature), the Bible and the Holy Spirit. Of the three, the Bible gives us the objective parameters by which we can understand the other two. Based on this revelation, we have a knowledge base from which we are able to know God and his ways. Here are the three important things we know.

1. Who is God?

Scripture teaches us that there is one living and true God. He is a person, is personal and is characterized by such attributes as spirit, knowledge, creativity, personality, free will, eternalness, dominion and self-consciousness. For his own purposes, God created the material universe and is actively involved in keeping it going as long as it suits his purposes. He has revealed himself to be perfect in every way, and has let us know that we should give him our highest love, gratitude and service.

Though there is one and only one God, he has revealed himself to mankind in three expressions – God the Father, Jesus Christ and the Holy Spirit. These three expressions of his personhood reveal specific attributes of his essence. At the same time, they do not indicate any division of his nature, his essence or his being.

As Father, God has revealed himself through his creative power and in the way he maintains the order of the material universe. By observing nature we can gain certain glimpses into his character. We can see that he is a God of order and that he expresses himself through the mechanism of cause and effect. Among other things, we can also recognize his creativity and concern for the created order.

He also displays his fatherly attributes in his relationship to mankind. This does not mean that every human being is related to him in a father-child relationship. It is possible for God to act with fatherly care, even toward those who do not establish a personal relationship with him. But there is the potential for individual humans to actually enter into a personal relationship with him. In that case, the father-child relationship becomes a personal reality. Individuals may choose to enter this relationship through faith in Jesus Christ. At that point, the interaction with God becomes personal rather than impersonal.

As Jesus Christ, God revealed himself in human flesh. Though he is often referred to in the New Testament as the Son of God or the Son of Man, he is, in his essence, God. In order to reveal himself in human form, it was necessary for him to put limits on himself, since material reality cannot hold the fullness of the personhood of God.

God's purpose in becoming a human was twofold. First, it was a way for him to reveal himself in a visible and tangible way to mankind. Since God, in his essence, is spirit, it is impossible for humans, who are confined to the material world, to understand everything about him. By becoming a human being, God was able to provide a concrete understanding of his character and his expectations. Secondly, his death on the cross and resurrection from the dead provided the means for mankind to overcome the bondage of sin and death. As humans, our sin against God causes us to deserve eternal separation from him. By his death and resurrection, Christ paid the penalty for our spiritual crimes, demonstrated his authority to offer forgiveness, and presented us with the opportunity to receive that forgiveness.

His conception was supernatural. He was miraculously conceived in Mary's womb as a work of God by means of the Holy Spirit, and was physically born in the land of Israel.

During his lifetime he perfectly lived out God's plan and provided a new level of revelation concerning how human beings should understand God and live life.

His death came about by execution on a Roman cross as a common criminal. This execution, though, was the means by which God provided the way to heaven for mankind. We are the ones who deserved the death penalty for our own sin. By offering himself as a sacrifice on the cross, Jesus substituted himself for those who are willing to accept it. On the third day after his death, he was bodily raised from the dead. Following that, he made appearances to his followers for a period of forty days. After that time, he rose to heaven and was elevated to the right hand of God where he serves as the intermediary between man and God. One day he will return to the earth in all of his power and glory to judge the world.

The third expression of God is the Holy Spirit. The Holy Spirit is not a separate entity from the Father and from Jesus Christ. He is, rather, another form that God has used to reveal himself to mankind. This whole idea of one God in three persons is one of the true mysteries of the Christian faith, but also helps us grasp at least some sense of how God interacts with mankind and with himself. In this form, God is able to interact with each individual human being on a direct and personal basis – all at the same time.

In the form of the Holy Spirit, God inspired men to write Scripture, and he continues to inspire individuals as they read that same scripture. By so doing, he makes it possible for people to understand the truth contained within it. As Holy Spirit, he also works personally and directly in the lives of individuals, and causes them to recognize their need for a relationship with himself.

2. What is a Human Being?

Mankind is a spiritual creature who inhabits a material body and who was created by a special act of God. He is different from all of the other living creatures which God created because of this spiritual essence. As a being who was created "in the image of God," humans possess the very characteristics that God himself possesses (things such as creativity, free will, self-consciousness, etc.).

Humans do not exhibit these characteristics to the same degree God does. But it does put us in the same "being" category with him. God is a person and his personal characteristics define his personhood. We are persons because God created us in his image with the characteristics of "personhood." We are persons because God is a person and he created us in his image, not the other way around.

Not only is mankind different in character from other creatures, but also different as it relates to God's purpose. Humanity was created for the purpose of personal fellowship with God.

God initially created the first man and woman innocent of sin and able to personally interact with himself without restriction. But by their own free will, they chose rebellion from God and fell from that original innocence. As a result of this choice, the loss of innocence was passed on to their children as an element of human nature. By this, humanity became corrupted and inclined toward sin and evil. This also created a gulf of separation between man and God.

On a personal level, individual humans do not have the internal power to bridge this gulf. It requires an act of God's grace to correct the problem. God provided the means for remedying the problem by the death and resurrection of Jesus Christ. It is up to each individual to freely choose to accept this remedy in order to restore fellowship with God.

3. What Comprises Salvation?

Salvation is the process by which individuals are able to solve the problem of man's separation from God. It is offered as a free gift to every person who willingly asks God for it based on the forgiveness provided through the death and resurrection of Jesus Christ. While salvation, in the macro sense, is a single element, we can observe how it plays itself out in three distinct stages of human existence. We experience it as a process because of the fact that we operate within the confines of material reality.

The first stage is often referred to as justification or the new birth. This takes place at a particular point in time. It happens when an individual specifically acknowledges and turns away from personal sin, and asks God's forgiveness based on the death and resurrection of Jesus Christ. The new birth happens by an act of faith whereby the individual acknowledges Christ as Savior and Lord. This represents the beginning point of a person's salvation, or personal relationship with God.

The second stage is called sanctification and represents the period of time between the moment a person receives Christ and physical death. During this stage of salvation, a believer is directed by God to willingly and actively work toward moral and spiritual perfection. This is not an unreasonable request because God himself, in the form of the Holy Spirit, attaches his life and power to the person who enters into relationship with him. This does not mean, however, that any individual has ever actually reached perfection in this life. But the power and the internal desire to move in that direction is present.

The third stage of salvation is called glorification. This stage begins at physical death when an individual's spirit is freed from the confines of the material world. At that point, the sin nature, which was part and parcel of the human body, is left behind, and the individual enters directly and eternally into the very presence of God.

Do You Know It?

The information above is the basic understanding of what witnessing involves and why it is important. If you have ever learned a witnessing method, this is the basic information that you learned inside of the package of your method. If you don't have this basic knowledge of the essentials of the Christian faith, it is impossible to share it with another person. For many people, it is a simple lack of knowledge of the facts that keeps them from sharing their faith with another person.

If you have not yet mastered this information, that is the place you have to start. You can't go any further until you do it. Don't wait any longer. Your ability to share a witness is too important to neglect mastering these fundamentals. Do what you have to do right now to get this under your belt.

But recognize, this is only the first step. There are some other issues you must take into account in order to become effective in sharing your faith with others.

Digging Deeper

1. If someone were to come up to you right now and ask you how to become a Christian, would you know what to tell them?

2. What is the essential nature of God?

3. What is the essential nature of a human being?

4. Summarize the full process of salvation.

As I interacted with Tom, he at first didn't want to share with me his belief system. He just wanted me to share mine. Certainly I was happy to do that, but it made it very difficult for me to know how I should frame my message to him. I didn't really know what he already understood about the Christian faith, so I struggled to find where to start with him. As it turned out, he did misunderstand many of the points I was trying to make and I had to keep giving him clarifications.

When I was finally able to get him to share his beliefs with me, he did it in a list of numbered points. His points actually contained most of the information I needed in order to understand him, but it was organized in a way that was not very systematic. To make sense of it all, I needed his beliefs to be a bit better organized.

To solve that problem, I took his points and reorganized them in a way that allowed me to systematically see what he believed about the essentials of his faith. Through that process, I was easily able to learn what he believed about God, man and salvation, and what authority he was basing his beliefs on.

Chapter 2
How Are Various Belief Systems Different?

When my wife and I went to Japan to serve as missionaries, we had opportunities to share Christ with various Japanese people that we met. But there were some things that were different about our witnessing experiences there than the way it was in America.

For instance, in America, I would often use Campus Crusade's Four Spiritual Laws pamphlet as a tool for my witness. That booklet was actually available in Japan, as well. In fact, it was produced in a fashion, that was helpful even for someone who did not have great Japanese language skills. It was bilingual with Japanese and English printed on facing pages. However, I never really had much success using it. It was a great idea, but there was a problem related to what the hearers understood about God.

In fact, every method that I ever learned and used in America had the same problem. It was not an issue of whether or not the translation was good or bad, it was a problem of concepts. It occurred because the Japanese were brought up under an entirely different worldview with a different understanding about the very nature of spiritual reality.

For instance, the first of the Four Spiritual Laws states, "God loves you and has a wonderful plan for your life." Now that is a great beginning if, when you read it, the person you are talking to has the same basic understanding about God that you have. But that was not the case in Japan. The most prominent religions in Japan are Shinto and Buddhism. In addition to that, there is a very strong Confucian underpinning to the culture, as well. And if that were not enough, there also exists a strong Naturalistic element.

The bottom line for witness is that their understanding of God is entirely different from what Christians believe. If you simply read, "God loves you and has a wonderful plan for your life," they would interpret that according to their understanding of God. What they would hear would be entirely different than what I meant. When I say, "God," I am referring to the one Creator God who is revealed in the Bible. When they use the word, they are thinking of one or more of the gods in the Japanese pantheon. Same word, different gods.

In order to be effective in my witness, I had to start at an entirely different place. I had to create a bridge between their understanding of God and what I wanted them to understand about the God of the Bible. The first thing I had to do with Japanese people was to help them come to a place where they understood that there is only one God. I then had to explain what he is like. Only when they had that understanding could I begin to move them along to a point that would allow them to respond to a gospel witness.

It used to be that American society was fairly homogenous in a spiritual sense. While not everyone necessarily believed the same thing, the huge majority did understand reality to be based on a Judeo-Christian worldview. That is, they believed that there was a single creator God who made things to be the way they are and who could be known, at least to some extent.

But things have changed radically. While the traditional understanding about God is still the majority view, there are two other factors that have come into play which have dramatically changed the spiritual landscape.

The first change is the result of a large influx of people from other countries who have brought their worldviews with them. While the new people themselves represent a large part of this change, the effect they are having on other Americans is also playing a role. As more people are exposed to these other worldviews, many are adopting them as their own, or at least accepting them as viable alternatives for understanding the way reality is structured.

The second change is a more global one that overlays what is already out there. A significant aspect of postmodern thought has to do with the acceptance of other points of view. This goes beyond simply having respect for people with other belief systems. It actually accepts every belief system as equally valid. It takes the approach that, "I have my beliefs which are good for me, but if you want to have a different belief system and it is good for you, then that is equally valid." The result of this mindset is that a large percentage of Americans no longer have an objective understanding of truth. It is relative to the person who holds the belief. Adding to the problem, many Christians have also bought into this way of thinking.

What Is Wrong with this Picture?

There is one significant problem with the postmodern approach. It is impossible to hold to it and be consistent. One of the principles of worldview is that each one explicitly excludes every other one. If the postmodernist belief is true, which asserts that every belief system is equally valid, then it is not true that Jesus Christ is the only way to get to God. If Hinduism or Islam is true, then Christianity is not. These different belief systems contradict one another at such a fundamental level that no two of them can be true at the same time.

There is something that is *the truth*. As Christians we believe that the teachings about God, man and salvation, as they are explained in the Bible, represent that objective truth. The teachings in the Bible not only give us insight and understanding about the essential elements of faith and the material universe, they also command us to share that truth with other people in an effort to bring them into a personal relationship with Christ.

In the past this was much easier than it is in our current day because now there are so many competing belief systems that we must engage. But the task is not hopeless. In fact, it is much easier than most might imagine.

Most people, who have an interest in engaging those with other philosophies and religions, feel that in order to do so, it is necessary to become an expert in apologetics and philosophy of religion. But that is simply not the case. Certainly every piece of knowledge you can gain about other belief systems will be a huge benefit. But there is a way to approach this topic that easily allows you to have the confidence to share the gospel with anyone. There is still a certain knowledge base that must be established. But that foundation relates to understanding belief systems in general rather than the memorization of a bunch of facts about various groups.

Getting at Worldview

The procedure we are going to look at for witnessing involves getting a grasp of worldview – the fundamental assumptions about the way reality is organized. Now, this may initially sound a bit philosophical and esoteric, but it is not nearly as daunting as you might think.

As you are probably aware, there are literally hundreds of different religions and philosophies in the world. Getting your mind wrapped around all of these without some kind of organizing principle is very difficult. But getting at it using a worldview approach makes the task much less complicated. The approach I have taken in this book organizes all belief systems around only four basic worldviews. Every religion, cult or philosophy emerges out of these four. It is not our intent, in this book, to delve deeply into the specifics of all of the religions, cults and philosophies. If you are interested in a deeper background about worldview, you might want to investigate my previous book, *Culture Wars*, and explore the resources that are posted on the MarketFaith Ministries website (www.marketfaith.org). It will, though, be helpful just to get a quick overview in order to have a sense of how this applies to the topic of our witness.

1. Naturalism

Basic Assumption: The only thing that exists is matter which is evolving and eternal.

Implications: When a human group forms, they decide, based on their own perceived needs, what kinds of values and behaviors will be useful for the survival of the group. If the situation changes, there is no compelling reason why the cultural elements can't also be changed. Morality is simply what the group wants it to be.

Belief Systems in this Category: Secular Humanism, Atheism, Agnosticism, Skepticism, Existentialism, Marxism, Positivism, and some forms of Postmodernism.

2. Animism

Basic Assumption: The universe contains both material and immaterial parts. Spirits exist in a separate place from physical beings, but they interact with each other in a symbiotic relationship.

Implications: The world and life are not moving toward a higher destination, so the tendency is simply to live life one day at a time and accept things the way they are. Left to themselves, Animistic cultures tend to remain living in primitive circumstances with very little societal advancement.

Belief Systems in this Category: Japanese Shinto, Witchcraft, Astrology, Fortune telling, Spiritism, Voodoo, and Native American Religions.

3. Far Eastern Thought

Basic Assumption: The cosmos is composed of an impersonal substance. Everything that exists is formed from that substance and is moving toward unity. God is everything and everything is god.

Implications: The primary impact of Far Eastern Thought on culture is to promote passivism. People should simply accept their station in life and live good enough to move to a higher form in their next life.

Belief Systems in this Category: Hinduism, Hare Krishna, Transcendental Meditation, Buddhism, Jainism, Sikhism, and Taoism.

4. Theism

Basic Assumption: There is an infinite and transcendent God who is Creator and Sustainer.

Implications: Theism basically lends itself to an impact on culture that is both moral and positive. But most forms result in a legalistic approach to living life and the development of culture. The moral order ought to be a certain way because it is written in "the law" or put forth by "the prophet." The way things ought to be are specifically prescribed by an outside authority.

Belief Systems in this Category: Christianity, Judaism, Islam, The Way International, The Family International, Jehovah's Witnesses, and Mormonism.

5. Hybrids

There is a group of belief systems that don't neatly fit into any of these. I call these hybrids because they take elements from two or more of the above worldviews and combine them. In actual fact, this can only be done by ignoring the inconsistencies that naturally arise when trying to merge multiple worldviews. That being said, there are a few which have become large enough to be considered as we think about how to witness. These include such groups as: New Age, Unitarian Universalist, Christian Science, The Unity School of Christianity, The Unification Church/Moonies, Satanism, Scientology, Confucianism, and Bahai.

Breaking Down a Worldview

In order to effectively break down a worldview, there is a series of questions that we must elicit the answers to. There are, actually, several ways to get at this, but the approach I like best is to use the seven worldview questions that Dr. James Sire shares in his groundbreaking book on worldview, *The Universe Next Door*. Here are the seven worldview questions and the kinds of answers that are possible from each one.

1. What is the nature of ultimate reality?
- There is no God.
- There is some kind of God.
- There are multiple Gods.
- God is personal.
- God is impersonal.

2. What is the nature of material reality?
- It is created or uncreated.
- It is orderly or chaotic.
- It is subjective or objective.
- It is personal or impersonal.
- It is eternal or temporal.

3. What is a human being?
- A human is a highly evolved biological machine.
- A human is a god or potential god.
- A human is one expression of the life energy which shifts forms through successive existences.
- A human is a being created by God.
- A human is a person made in the image of God.

4. What happens to a person at death?
- He/she ceases to exist.
- He/she transforms to a higher state.
- He/she reincarnates.
- He/she departs to a shadowy existence on "the other side."
- He/she enters into the spiritual realm (heaven, hell, or other place) based on how life was lived on earth.
- He/she enters directly into heaven.

5. Why is it possible to know anything at all?
- Consciousness and rationality developed through a long process of evolution.
- There is no "reason" for us to know anything. That is just the nature of our existence.
- Knowledge is an illusion.
- Humans are made in the image of God who has knowledge.

6. How do we know what is right and wrong?
- Right and wrong are strictly products of human choice.
- Right and wrong are determined by what feels good.
- A sense of right and wrong was an evolutionary development as a survival mechanism for the species.
- Right and wrong are learned by experience as we discover what pleases the gods.

- Right and wrong are a prescribed set of rules dictated by God.
- We are made in the image of God whose character is good and who has revealed what is right and wrong.

7. *What is the meaning of human history?*
- There is no innate meaning to human history. Meaning is what humans make it to be.
- Time is an illusion.
- Meaning comes as we realize the purpose of the gods.
- Meaning comes when we discover and fulfill the purpose of God.

Something is Truth

So far we have looked at the possible worldviews and have laid out a means to evaluate them. Before we move on, though, there is one more issue that needs to be addressed. There is, and can only be, one belief system that actually lines up with the way reality is organized. As Christians, we believe that the Christian faith is that system.

This is not to say that we have the capability to understand every part of it. In fact, there are many aspects of reality that are well beyond our ability to know – particularly things related to the realm of the spirit. That being said, there are some things we can know because God thought it important enough to reveal it to us.

The things that God especially wanted us to be aware of relate to who he is, the nature of a human being and the way we can know him. He used several means to give this revelation. First, he revealed himself through the created order. Secondly, he revealed himself through individuals whom he chose as messengers. These messengers have left a written record of that revelation - the Bible. Thirdly, he revealed himself by taking on the form of a human being - the man Jesus Christ.

Finally, he revealed himself by making it possible for humans to interact directly with him Spirit to spirit - by his Holy Spirit.

In order to try and make this distinction clear, I have coined a new term to represent this belief system – Relational Revelation. This is actually not something new. Rather, it is the form of Theism that represents Biblical Christianity. Relational Revelation represents "the Truth." It is the belief system that matches up most closely with the way we, as human beings, live and experience life in the created order. This belief system is characterized by the following.

Basic Assumption: There is a personal, infinite, transcendent God who is Creator and Sustainer, and who has revealed himself in the Bible.

Implications: Relational Revelation lends itself to an impact on culture that is both moral and positive. It does all of this in a way that puts a priority on a personal relationship with God as the motivation for fulfilling his purposes. It is not just the end result that matters. The means by which the outcome is brought about is also vital. The means are conveyed by personal instruction from God to individual human beings.

What All of this Means

Let us be clear on one thing before we move forward. While we don't have to learn all of the aspects of every religion and philosophy in order to engage people with other belief systems, there are some things we do have to become familiar with and learn. Learning to witness effectively is not strictly an intellectual process, but there is an aspect where it is necessary to engage the mind.

If you are serious about your desire to stand with confidence in your faith as you live your life and engage the world, it is not appropriate to take the lazy person's way out. It is not right to look at the task and consider it to be too complicated or difficult. When God charged us with the task to be witnesses to the world, he didn't say, "Do it if it is convenient." He just said, "Do it." What we are considering here is simply a tool to help you take that command seriously.

What all of this gives us is simply a way to evaluate and compare worldviews. By asking the worldview questions, we can find out what another person believes at a level that allows us to engage them in a meaningful way. Once we have a grip on our own and another person's worldview positions, we can begin to show them how their position will not lead them to God, and how our Christian faith does.

Digging Deeper

1. Do you believe that the Christian teachings concerning the objective reality of God are true? Why or why not?

2. Consider each of the four foundational worldviews. What issues arise for each one that can be problematic in its claim to be the truth about the nature of ultimate reality?

3. Why is it important for us to be able to understand and compare the basic assumptions of each of the worldviews?

In my interaction with Tom, a very interesting exchange occurred on a couple of different occasions. At the very beginning of our dialogue, he came up with a number of statements that we might agree on as the basis for our discussion. In a general sense, we were actually able to do this. However, even within those statements there were things that I knew we would have to clarify. For instance, we both believe in one God. The problem is, we do not agree on the nature of that God.

When I began to challenge his understanding of God, he got upset with me because I was, in his mind, challenging something we had already agreed to. His idea was that if we had agreed to it, it was not a topic for discussion (as if the points of agreement covered every element of the nature of God).

In fact, God exists as a real objective person. He has certain characteristics and doesn't have others. When I began to understand the true nature of God's personhood and realized that I could know him and interact with him like a real person, it changed my life. It also changed the way I related to him.

As I discussed this with Tom, a general agreement about the fact that there is only one God was not enough. The God he described was not capable of the kind of relationship I had already come to know.

Chapter 3
Your Understanding of God Determines Your Effectiveness

From my teenage years I have been a big fan of Glen Campbell. If you are a bit younger than I am, you may not even know who he is. But back in the day, he was one of the hottest singers around. His biggest hits came in the 1960s and 70s. He sang and toured with the Beach Boys for a short time, and has done session work with some of the biggest names in the music industry.

In his heyday, he had many huge hits, and was so popular that he even had his own TV show and starred in movies. I really don't hear of him much any more, but I still love to listen to his music.

Because I am a big fan, I have made the effort to learn a little bit about his life. I know that he grew up very poor in Arkansas, the son of a share cropper. As a youngster, he had a talent for music and was encouraged in it. He had an uncle who was a good guitarist and who spent time teaching him to play. His uncle later took Glen on the road and they began to play in whatever bars and other small local venues that would hire them.

As they did this, Glen began to meet some people who had connections in the music industry, and who encouraged him to go to Hollywood. When he finally decided to make that move, he met some folks who had the influence to get him work as a studio musician. Gradually, as his career developed, he began to record some of his own music until finally, in the 1960s, he hit the big time.

But his life was not all good. He took several opportunities to try and ruin the life that he had developed. In the course of his career he got involved in drugs and went through several divorces. He even spent time in jail.

But after the roughest portions of his life, he really did try to pull himself together. He got married to a woman who helped him get off of the drugs and alcohol that were destroying his life, and worked on getting his spiritual life straightened out. He even recorded some Christian albums and won a couple of Dove awards.

I really do like Glen Campbell and his music. But there is something else you need to know. I have never met him. Even though I have listened to his music for years and have made the effort to get to know some things about him, I don't know him personally. I can enjoy his music, but can't enjoy him.

Does that make any difference? Absolutely! Knowing about someone's life makes it possible to satisfy a certain curiosity. And it allows a person the opportunity to learn some life lessons from another. But that is very different from a personal relationship. Knowing someone personally allows you to learn directly from them. When I only know about someone, I have to filter the information I discover through my own experience. When I know them directly, they can explicitly pour their experience, and their life, into mine.

Sad to say, there are many Christians who know a lot about God simply because they read his book and listen to other people talk about him. They have a great respect for him and even allow his teachings to have an impact on their lives. But many of those people don't really know him personally. Some actually have met him, but don't continually spend time together with him so that their lives can be shaped by his training.

Up until now, the things we have dealt with have mostly involved the intellect – things you have to know in order to give an effective verbal witness. But, there is another element that may be a bigger challenge to our personal witness than not knowing the necessary content. In fact, this may be the reason why so many Christians don't ever even make the effort to learn the content, even though they know they should be out sharing their faith.

The topic of this chapter may, at first, seem a little bit on the deep end. But hopefully you will soon recognize that this is one of the most practical aspects of witness you will ever encounter. It directly determines the way you go about your own personal evangelistic activity.

Here is the principle. ***You live your life based entirely on your personal experience of reality.*** Now that seems simple and straightforward enough, right? After all, what other possibilities are there? In fact, it probably seems so obvious that you are wondering, "Well, duh! Why did you even say something like that?"

Now, before you get too put out with me, let's look at the implications of that statement. You might end up changing your tune a little bit.

I am going to list a few questions and I want you to answer them to yourself with brutal honesty. You need to recognize something before you do it, though. If you simply skim through the questions and read them without taking the time to answer them as I asked, you will miss the entire point of this chapter. Our point here is to make a distinction between intellectual knowledge and experiential knowledge. It is an utterly profound distinction. If you skip this little exercise, you will completely bypass the experiential element we are trying to get at. Okay, here goes.

- Do you believe in Jesus Christ?
- Do you believe that when Jesus commissioned Christians to share the gospel, that he was serious that all believers have that responsibility, including yourself?
- How seriously do you take that responsibility for yourself? How often do you share your faith with people who do not know Christ?
- Do you feel competent to share your faith with nonbelievers? If someone came up to you right now and asked you how to become a Christian, could you share the message?
- When you get into a conversation about faith or religion outside of a Christian gathering, do you get uncomfortable or uptight?
- Would you characterize your level of confidence about sharing your faith with a nonbeliever as extremely confident, somewhat confident or not at all confident?

I hope that you have truly been honest with your answers. Now, I am going to be brutal with my assessment. If you are anything but extremely confident, your personal experience of reality concerning God may be your problem.

The Key to Effective Witness

I want to make a distinction here that is vital to our ability to become effective witnesses. There is a massive difference between intellectual belief and experiential belief. Go take a survey of random people in your church and ask them if they believe in God. It would probably be quite shocking to find even one who says they do not. Otherwise, why would they even attend? Next, ask them if they sit down and have a conference with God every day to plan out how to accomplish his purpose for their day. Your response from most people will be for them to look at you like you are crazy.

Why is that? Because most people, even church people, don't conceive of their lives that way. For most, God is a somewhat abstract, relatively impersonal being who is basically the big Santa Claus in the sky, and who exists to make their life run better. In actual fact, God is a real, objective person with whom we can interact concretely. And this real God has a tangible and specific plan for our lives that he wants us to live by. This second understanding of God is exactly the opposite of the first.

So what is the problem? Every individual interacts with God based on who they understand him to be. Do you sit at the table with God and plan out your life strategy? Or do you plan out your life and ask God to bless it and give you stuff to make things easier?

For some people, thinking of God as an actual, objective presence is too much like a child having an imaginary friend. Fun or comforting to imagine, but not really real. The difference here is that even though God is unseen with the physical eyes, he is objectively real and he is personal. Intellectually, most Christians acknowledge this reality. Most, though, do not experience their relationship with God this way.

There are various reasons why this is the case, but all of the specific reasons tend to boil down to one cause – selfishness. That's right! We want to live our lives according to our own plans and desires. It is much easier to do that and ask God's blessing on our desires than to turn our lives over to him and let him be the navigator.

What do we have to do to change our perspective so that God's plans become primary in our lives? We have to:

· Consider our lives to be God's property. We have to be willing to completely let go of our own ambitions, figure out God's direction, and channel our ambitious fires to accomplish his purposes – no matter where it leads. Are you *excited* to head in any direction God leads no matter what it might be?

· Consider our material possessions to be God's property. We have to understand that we don't have any money. It is all

God's. We must then discern how God wants it to be invested. Part of the investment will be to take care of our personal and family needs. Other parts will be to accomplish other purposes through our lives. Are you *excited* to discern how God wants to use the resources he has put in your hands?

- Consider our vocation to be God's property. I have met so many people who were not willing to give their lives fully to God because they were afraid he would call them to be a preacher or a missionary to Africa, or something like that. The fact is, God only calls a very small percentage of people to enter those kinds of leadership positions. The percentages say that any particular individual will not be led that way. But that is entirely irrelevant. The person fully given over to God doesn't care. Are you *excited* to find the vocation God wants you to pursue in order to be a witness to the people you meet in that context?

- Consider our morality to be at God's discretion. God does have a standard of morality that he has established. Many people look at that standard as an external set of rules. If that is what it is to you, it is an indication that your relationship with God is faulty. Everyone who has a personal and concrete interaction with God is so in love with him that they would not even want to do things that offend him. Are you *excited* to know what kind of lifestyle pleases God, and do you live fully in it?

We could go on and on with the list. We could talk about how we take care of our physical bodies, what kind of relationships we engage in, how we spend our time and so on. But the point is, it is all about God, not about us. It is all about actively interacting with a real and personal God who loves us, has a plan for our lives, and wants to guide us to accomplish *his* purpose in the world.

How Real Is It?

So now we are back to the one essential question. How experientially real is God to you? It is certainly possible to periodically work a verbal witness off of your intellect. You can develop a formula that goes: 1) I know what God wants me to do, 2) I will learn how to present the plan of salvation, and 3) I will force myself to do it. The only problem is, this mechanical approach is fake. Sure God can use it. He is not going to abandon someone who needs him just because the messenger hasn't got his or her act together. But it is very difficult to maintain your enthusiasm over an extended period of time when you are only operating out a sense of duty rather than out of relationship.

But if you really know God in a personal relationship and are actively and concretely engaged in that relationship, day in and day out, you are no longer sharing a "plan of salvation" when you share the gospel. At that point it becomes an act of introducing your friend Jesus to your friends Bill and Mary.

So, how real is God to you? Are you experiencing him right now with you? Do you feel comfortable turning to him and asking his opinion about what you are doing? Have you developed a communication channel with him so you can experience his response when you ask? And when you ask, are you close enough to him to understand his answer?

God is a real, objective person. Until your relationship with him becomes experiential (as opposed to merely intellectual), you will be relegated to working for God out of a sense of duty. When you are able to work from the relationship, your witness will truly become exciting.

Digging Deeper

1. What do you think about your answers to the questions in this chapter that related to the intellectual and experiential understanding of your faith?

2. What do you need to do in your life to make God primary and your own desires secondary?

3. Experientially, how real is God to you?

At this point you might be interested to know how I met Tom. One day I read an article in our local newspaper about how some folks did not like the fact that the city commission began their meeting with prayer. I didn't agree with the point of view of the writer and wrote a letter to the editor. When the paper printed it, they also included my e-mail address and several people e-mailed me directly with their opinion of my letter. Tom was one of those.

Our relationship lasted several weeks as we e-mailed back and forth. This relationship was strange in some respects, but it did provide me the opportunity to share a witness. I don't know if Tom will ever let go of his belief and embrace the gospel. But if he does, I have the pleasure of knowing that my witness will be a part of the puzzle that helped him understand it.

Chapter 4
Your Understanding of People Determines Your Effectiveness

Several years ago I counseled a couple who were having some very serious marital problems. It seems that the man had caught the woman visiting one of her former boyfriends. When this happened, he felt completely betrayed and decided to leave her. It really broke his heart.

For the woman, though, it was just a little fling, and she obviously didn't think it was nearly as big a deal as her husband did. That being said, she really didn't want it to break up her marriage, so she contacted me to counsel with them.

The husband had already pretty much decided that he was not going to live with someone who would betray him like that, and he wasn't really interested in coming to see me. But somehow she was able to talk him into it.

I wish I could say that this had a happy ending, but under the circumstances it was virtually impossible. When they came to my office and we began to talk, the woman began to say she didn't want to break up and that what he thought was a fling was nothing more than her seeing an old friend. She began to accuse him of just being overly jealous.

She was actually pretty convincing until he began probing her with specific questions. She finally had to admit that not only had she had an affair with this other man, but that even as we sat there and talked she was lying. She just proved once again that she could not be trusted with his heart. He could not bring himself to go back to her.

Relationships are, in many ways, very fragile things. They are built on trust and loyalty. As long as the trust exists, the relationship can exist. The really good news is that trust can deepen. And as people come to the place where they are able to trust each other more, they become more able to share intimate parts of their lives. But it works the other way, too, like the couple above. If the trust is broken, people become less willing to share the deepest elements of their lives.

If we want to be effective at being the messenger who is able to share the gospel of Jesus Christ with other people, we must have the kind of relationship with God which gives us first hand experiential knowledge of his great love. That is what the whole last chapter was about. But there is another set of relationships that we must also develop. We must develop relationships with other people so that they will trust us to talk with them about one of the most intimate and sensitive aspects of human life – their immortal spirit.

This kind of relationship is becoming more and more difficult to cultivate. Research that has been done over the last several decades indicates a trend of increasing isolation. People are allowing fewer and fewer confidants into their lives. Part of the problem relates to changes in technology which allow people to live and work in ways that don't require the same kind of interpersonal relationships that used to be necessary.

These days we can work at remote locations by ourselves via computer. Besides our work, technology channels us into entertainment activities that focus on a TV or video screen. Even if we are in the same room with other people we do not interact with them as much.

But it is not just technology. Even our living circumstances cause us to be more isolated. We tend to be so busy with our kid's, and our own, activities that we are never in one place long enough to develop deep friendships. And our homes and communities are increasingly set up in ways that keep us isolated from our neighbors.

If we want to become effective in witness, we have to somehow overcome these barriers and do something to develop relationships which allow for it. There are two things that we need to reconcile within ourselves if we are going to make it happen. First, we must learn to have God's point of view concerning people who don't know him. Secondly, we have to learn how to take some initiative.

God's Point of View

The perspective we have on life is very important. Our attitude, and the things we focus on in our lives, are dependent upon it. Our natural tendency is to look at, and live, life from our own personal perspective. But God did not make life to revolve around us. He made it to revolve around himself. If we really want to get fulfillment in life, we have to start where God starts. As it relates to humanity, that starting place is his love. God loves everyone and wants a relationship with each individual human being.

Unfortunately, there are many people in the world who don't know God's love. As a result, they are headed to an eternity separated from him if they don't turn to Christ.

This is where we have the opportunity to intersect with what God is trying to do in the world. In fact, God has commissioned us to be his instruments to accomplish his purpose. Since we have experienced his work in our own lives, we are witnesses of the good news of how God is able to change a person's life. Now it is up to us to share that good news with those who do not know him.

Intentional Witness

But as we have already explored in other areas, simple intellectual assent is not enough to generate action. We have to exert some energy if we want something to be accomplished. In the case of our witness, we have to take the initiative to interact with other people.

Now this is easier for some than for others. Some people are just naturally outgoing and make friends easily. Virtually everywhere they go, they leave a trail of new people they have met. But being an extrovert is not a requirement for making friends. There is no law that says how many people you have to meet. It just requires that you be willing to step up to the plate to create friendships whenever that opportunity presents itself. This is not a strange thing. Even the most introverted people have some friends.

That being said, most people tend more toward isolation. But as Christians, we have to buck the trend of focusing inwardly. The easiest way for you to do this is to open yourself up and let people know you. You don't have to be an extrovert to do this. You only have to be transparent. When people recognize that you are open to them, they will naturally begin to connect with you.

Once we have personally made the determination to open ourselves up to others, we have to take steps to identify the specific people we need to witness to. Don't take this to be an artificial action. Not everyone is going to be attracted to a relationship with you. And anyway, it is impossible for you to verbally give a witness to everyone. That is why God has placed Christians in so many different places. Everyone has their own circle of influence. If you are open to relationships, people will be attracted to you and opportunities will come.

But there is one last thing. We have to make an intentional effort to become friends with those God places in our path. We can't always just be in "waiting" mode. Some people will not begin to open up to you until you take some initiative toward them. This doesn't mean to attack them with the gospel. It simply means to go out of your way to become their friend. Once you do that, the witnessing opportunity will emerge in due time.

Do Your Part

Everything that happens related to God's purposes is related to relationship. Our relationship with God must be in the right place before we will have the personal motivation to act on his behalf.

But relationship has to be central in the other direction, too. We have to develop relationships with people. We then become the bridge upon which individuals have the opportunity to meet God.

Digging Deeper

1. What does it mean in practical terms when we say, "Christians need to look at the world through God's eyes?"

2. Can you make a list of ten people that you know who are not believers in Christ?

3. Think of a particular individual that you know who does not know Christ. What practical things can you do to bring an intentional and effective witness to that person?

Part II
How to Witness to a Non-Christian Based on Worldview

When I was growing up it was rather unusual to meet many people from other cultures. Certainly there were foreigners around, but they were mostly affiliated with the university and did not mix very much with the general public in the places I frequented. The places in America where there were recognizable populations from other cultures were typically small pockets in some of the larger cities.

That is not the case any more. There are large numbers of people from other cultures just about everywhere, even in small town America.

Also, when I was growing up, most Americans considered themselves to be Christians. Even people who did not attend church still identified themselves with the Christian faith. Surveys indicate that the majority of Americans still have that tendency, but there are a couple of very significant differences. One is that the percentage is down from previous years. The other difference is that even many of those who consider themselves to be Christians don't see the moral values of Christianity to be absolute in the way they used to be thought of.

When I served as a missionary in Japan, the people I wanted to witness to had an entirely different way of thinking about morality and theology than those I grew up with in America. As a result, I had to interact with them in a different way. When I talked about God to a Japanese person, I had to first define who the God was I was talking about. They had an entirely different concept. In America, when I mentioned God, everyone knew I was talking about the God of the Bible.

America is different now. It seems that more and more it is necessary to interact with non-believing Americans in the same way I had to interact with the Japanese.

Chapter 5
Think Like a Missionary

The last formalized witness training I participated in was a two-day workshop. This program was a "new" methodology created by a pastor who had developed it for his church. It was designed to take advantage of a church's Sunday School program in order to get people connected with the church once they came to know the Lord. It was also designed to create a multiplication effect as more and more people would participate in the program over time. During the time period when I participated in this training, it was being heavily promoted on a national scale.

The system was actually a fairly good one as far as systems go. It was built on five points that were associated with scripture verses. These verses were designed to lead a person from an initial point of contact to a call to commitment. It covered all of the points that a person needs to know in order to make a decision to accept or reject Christ. The two days of classes were set up to help us memorize the presentation and motivate us to use it.

In order to learn how to use this method in a practical situation, the church where the training was held gathered together a bundle of cards with the names and addresses of people who had visited the church over the last several months. They then handed out the names and had us go do cold call witnessing to these people using the new method.

Following that, we returned to the church and debriefed the experience.

There were actually several good reports of people inviting Christ into their lives. And in general, the seminar was a pleasant experience. But from an overall perspective it seems that the method has had rather mixed results. Many churches that participated in the program had some good initial success. But the multiplication effect rarely lasted more than two or three cycles.

There are several reasons why programs like this tend to dwindle down over time, but the main problems relate to the things we have already been talking about. Many people doing the witnessing operated out of a sense of duty, rather than from a relationship foundation. And, even with the training, some of the people who were witnessed to did not share a common worldview with the presenter, and the experience was uncomfortable.

The example above is the story of my most recent witness training. But the fact is, all of the traditional witness training that I have ever participated in has treated the process of sharing the gospel in almost exactly the same way. The goal is to learn a skill or technique rather than learn how to engage a relationship.

Typically a method involves two parts. First, there is a core of material that must be memorized. This usually consists of a number of Bible verses which explain what the Bible says about entering into a relationship with Christ. The second part is a system into which the Bible verses are inserted. The system is designed to create a cohesive and understandable presentation.

Most of these systems include three parts: 1) an introductory phase where you engage the person, 2) a part where you share and explain the Bible verses, and 3) a concluding part where you try to bring the person to a decision. The typical methodology is for the Christian to find a venue to share this presentation, then go for the jugular all in one fell swoop. At the end, an individual typically either makes a decision to accept Christ or reject him.

First let me say that it is very helpful to have a memorized system in our repertoire so that when the opportunity presents itself we are able to tell people how they can receive Christ. I believe that every Christian ought to have that basic knowledge. My beef is not with having a system that we can use to share Christ.

That being said, I think we destroy most of our opportunities to be effective when we package our witness into a one-shot opportunity. There may be those rare times when it all happens that way. But for the most part, our best opportunities do not, and cannot, unfold in that manner. There are several reasons for this.

The most important reason is because the most profound and powerful sharing opportunities happen in the context of more long term relationships. One shot presentations which demand an immediate decision bring the whole process to an end when the presentation is completed. If a person accepts Christ, you may have the opportunity to jump on that and help them get connected to a church. But if they reject him, the game is over. They have already told you they don't want what you have offered, and most of the time it is extremely difficult to ever even bring up the topic again.

A second reason is that most people need more time to process information that is so deep, profound, and life altering. A call for a person to commit his or her life to Christ is not just a request for an intellectual assent to a proposition. It is a call to a profound life change. The implications go to the very core of a person's understanding of who they are and how they live life. Many people who are pushed to make a firm decision before they have had the chance to process what this really means for their lives, will fall away very quickly. I have seen it happen many times. If they are truly ready to make a decision, I don't believe they should delay. But if they are not, there needs to be a way to discern this and keep the door open until they are prepared to make a positive decision.

A third important reason is that many of the people who need a witness require a different starting place than our system allows. All of the systems that I am familiar with start with the assumption that the person receiving the witness already has the same understanding of God as the one giving the witness. That used to be pretty much the case in America, but no longer. More and more the gods of other religions, and the belief systems of other philosophies, are the default beliefs of people you run into. If you simply assume that those you are talking to already know what you are talking about when you speak of God, you may be way off base and your witness total nonsense to them.

Our society is no longer as homogenous as it once was. And we can no longer give our witness as if it were. Rather than the narrow systems approach that we have traditionally used, we now need a broader approach which allows us to assess where a person is in their understanding of God. This allows us to start with what they already understand. Then we can appropriately bring them to the understanding that there is one God who is the Creator and Sustainer of the universe, who is personal, and who desires a dynamic relationship with us individually.

This broader approach takes advantage of the tools that missionaries have had to use over the years to engage people with other belief systems. It involves understanding the principles of worldview and using those principles to engage people in a way that brings them to a comprehension of the truth. Let's now take the opportunity to establish an approach as to how we can make that happen in our personal witness.

Digging Deeper

1. What are the issues that make you uncomfortable when you think about the prospect of witnessing to someone?

2. What do you think would make you more at ease in that situation?

3. What do you need to do to put yourself in a position to be at ease giving a witness?

As a public speaker I have had opportunities to make presentations to a whole host of different kinds of audiences. Many of the audiences I address are groups I have never been in front of before. I don't know them and they don't know me. This fact presents a challenge because speaking to an audience is much like having a conversation with an individual. Some are much easier to engage than others.

It is interesting to see how different groups have very different personalities. Some groups have a lot of extraverted people. Those groups tend to be easy to speak to because they identify with new people quickly and easily. Other audiences, though, have a lot of introverts. These groups tend to be much more difficult to address because they don't quickly let new people into their lives.

Whenever I do a presentation, I do everything I can to establish some rapport with the audience as quickly as possible. If I am able, I even mix and mingle with the people before I ever get in front of the room. The better the relationship I am able to establish, the more willing people are to listen to, and heed, what I have to say.

Chapter 6
Think Relationship First

How important is perspective? In many ways your perspective about an activity is more fundamental than the actual activity itself.

As an author, I spend a lot of time at my word processor. To some, being an author probably seems quite glamorous. I must admit it is quite a thrill for me to see my work in print. It is also quite exciting when people come up to me and tell me that they really like my writing. But I can tell you, the process of writing can also be quite tedious. From the beginning step to finally having a published work in hand can take anywhere from several months to several years. There are so many steps to go through.

You must start by deciding what you want to write about, then put it down in outline form. Following that you have to flesh out the outline, then make it more readable by inserting appropriate illustrations. Once you have your basic material, you then have to go back through and edit. To do a good job you may have to read through and rewrite dozens of times.

When you finally get the content finished, it is then necessary to make sure that the cover design (front, back and spine) is just right. If you don't already have a publisher, you next have to decide how you want to go about getting it printed, and select a good company. Then comes the marketing

– a major undertaking all its own. The whole process can be quite daunting.

For me, the middle part of the writing process tends to be the most tedious. It is necessary to get highly focused on finding good illustrations and trying to figure out a good way to turn a phrase – and frankly, sometimes I just get tired of it. At that point, I have to refocus or I will simply give it up.

It is impossible not to be focused on the particular point you are working on at any given moment. But specific points in the middle of a big picture mean nothing in and of themselves. My personal refocus requires that I step back and see the big picture again. Why did I want to write the book in the first place? What is the big point I am trying to make, and how will it help my readers? It is the big picture that is exciting for me, not the details that make it up. When I get sucked into the details, I quickly lose the joy of my craft.

This very thing happens, too, when we think about the witnessing process. It is not the mastering of a procedure that is exciting or important about giving a witness. Who cares if you are able to memorize and master a witnessing system? Other people don't care, and it will become boring to you, too, if you lose the context of why you do it. God wants to change people's lives – and he wants to use you as a part of the process. Delivering a message is satisfying. Watching someone's life change before your very eyes is thrilling.

But it is not just the process itself that requires a proper perspective. We need to have the right way to look at the essence of witnessing itself. The tendency for most people is to look at it simply as an event that we participate in at a particular moment in time. But with that perspective, all we have are incidents that occur from time to time which we complete and are finished with. Once done, we have no more responsibility. Even though we probably realize that the process isn't *exactly* that way, or at least shouldn't be, with an event mentality it is difficult to see the bigger picture. Instead of thinking of it in terms of an event, we should be thinking of it in the context of an ongoing relationship.

As it relates to problem solving, the mindset of most Americans leads us to see a problem, figure out how to solve it, and attack it head on. Once we get the problem solved, we simply move on to the next one. That mentality usually serves us well as we try to grow our businesses, overcome obstacles and move forward with our lives.

But it is not necessarily the best approach for developing relationships – especially with people who have different beliefs than our own. Generally, people are not subject to manipulative processes in the arena of beliefs. Though it might be possible to use a slick system and actually talk someone into converting to your belief system for a time, there will generally come a point when they recognize that they have been manipulated and will rebel by no longer trusting you, and/or by simply ending the relationship.

When we are thinking about our witness, we need to create a new mindset. We need to establish an environment where people have the opportunity to hear our beliefs and watch our lives. In that context they have the time to process it for their own situation. It is very rare that any person would hear the gospel for the very first time and be willing to simply accept it. It happens occasionally, but it is the exception rather than the rule.

By the way, this is not something that is limited to our spiritual development. It is simply a fact that the profound things that happen in our lives take time. A reporter once asked Sam Walton how he achieved "overnight success." He replied, "It took twenty years to become an overnight success." Whether it is learning and processing the things we need for success in business, or the things we need to understand about God, there is normally a period of time that is necessary to work through it all.

If you have ever witnessed to someone and they did accept Christ on that first witness, there is a great chance that your presentation is not the first time they have heard it. They have probably been influenced growing up by family members, had contact over the years with Christian friends, experienced the witness of other people, and no telling what else.

Think about it. When you share the gospel, you are asking people to totally reorient their lives. It takes time for individuals to process that kind of information and understand all of the implications. If you truly want to be effective, you have to put yourself in a position to be around them for a long enough period of time that they are able to hear the message and see it consistently played out in your life. You have to keep it before them long enough for it to finally make sense to them.

Think relationship first, not method, system or event. And don't make their acceptance of Christ the condition for your friendship. You need to have relationships with people who are not Christians. Those are the only ones you will ever be able to lead to Christ. If you are faithful and consistent as a friend, there will come a time when you will be able to share. And if they don't accept Christ immediately, you are still their friend and will have other opportunities.

Digging Deeper

1. What relationships do you already have which you could use as a bridge for witness?

2. Who do you know who is not a Christian and with whom you could begin a deeper relationship?

3. Are you willing to intentionally create a relationship with someone who is not a Christian and cultivate that relationship for as much as two years or more in order to share Christ with them?

I once got into a conversation with a Jehovah's Witness. Sometimes they can be a little bit coy about how they initiate their interaction with you. Many of them will not tell you right off the bat that they are Jehovah's Witnesses because they know that many people will immediately cut off the conversation.

Initially this fellow was taking that approach with me. He did, though, make several provocative comments as he began his witness to me. His comments made me suspect that he was a member of that group, but I needed to be sure before I began talking with him about specific issues. I didn't want to be in a position where I was saying things that would not be relevant. But since he did not identify his beliefs I was stymied.

So I did the only thing I knew to do. I directly asked him what belief system he was coming from. Once he finally identified himself as a Jehovah's Witness, I was then able to engage him intelligently and give a witness back to him.

Chapter 7
Elicit Their Beliefs - Ask the Seven Worldview Questions

Virtually every day the press secretary for the President of the United States stands before the media and conducts his daily press briefing. The format is fairly straightforward. The press secretary stands behind a podium at the front of the room and begins with an overview of the president's schedule. He then goes on and shares any comments he wishes to make about ongoing events or issues that the president is involved in. The press corps sits in chairs facing him and, at the appropriate time, begins to ask questions related to any issue that they have a particular interest in.

What particular questions do they ask? Well, each day the members of the media have their own agendas related to stories and issues they think their readers and listeners want to know about. To take care of their agendas, they ask specific questions related to those topics. There are plenty of other questions they could ask about all sorts of other issues. But on any given day, they only ask the ones that they need the answers to concerning their stories. For instance, if they are doing a story on peace in the Middle East, they don't spend a lot of time asking questions about how the Federal Reserve is handling domestic interest rates. Rather, they focus on the events of the Middle East and how the president is dealing with them.

If your purpose in making a relationship with someone is to ultimately have the opportunity to share the gospel, there are certain things you are going to have to get around to asking. Certainly you will talk about a lot of other things in the course of the relationship – many of them having nothing at all to do directly with the gospel message itself. But like the reporters above, you have an agenda that you are working on. And at some point it will be necessary to find out the kind of information that helps you effectively share the gospel with your friend.

The specific information you need to elicit relates directly to their beliefs about God, the material world, mankind, the afterlife, morality, knowledge and meaning – the seven worldview questions that were discussed in chapter two. Knowing this kind of information will allow you to talk about your faith in a way that makes sense to them. For instance, if you begin by talking about God as if he is personal but your friend doesn't even believe in God, you will be dismissed right away. You will have to somehow bring your friend around to the possibility that there may be a God before he or she will even be willing to listen to you talk about what God might be like. You need to understand their worldview so you can create conversations that allow them to take you seriously.

How to Use the Questions

We have already looked at the questions that need to be asked, so we will not go over that again here. If you need to refresh your memory, you may want to reread chapter two. What we want to do here is to consider exactly how to go about asking the questions. We have to be sure that we ask them in a way that is not forced. If you just begin to pound away with hard-hitting questions, it may not fit very nicely into the context of your relationship. Remember, these questions are not designed to be a formula. You can't just work your way

ELICIT THEIR BELIEFS - ASK THE SEVEN WORLDVIEW QUESTIONS

through them and end up with a great witness. Rather, they are designed to elicit information which will help you become more able to effectively share your witness in the context of a relationship.

Of course it would be easier to just get to the point and start asking the questions one after the other. And there may be some instances where that might be possible. If you create a relationship that will support it and can steer a conversation in a way that allows it, maybe you can pull it off like that.

But in most cases, relationships simply don't work that way. Typically, the most natural thing is to elicit your friend's answers over a period of time. Each question deals with an element of belief and life. You learn about those things as a part of learning more about the person. One day you will talk about God and find out what they believe about him. Another time you will talk about the nature of the physical universe. At another opportunity you will talk about the foundation of morality. Let's just consider a couple of possibilities of how this might play out.

On a Monday morning you may be talking with your friend around the coffee pot and ask a simple question related to what they did over the weekend. In the course of that conversation they may drop a hint that they went to church or did not go to church. Perhaps they are not Christian and went to their synagogue, mosque or temple. Maybe they don't even believe in God and went fishing. If they bring up any of this, you can probe a little around the edges about things that will give you clues to what they believe about God.

And, since you asked about their weekend, it will be natural for them to ask you about yours, or for you to just start talking about what you did. In doing that, you can share about your participation in worship and how meaningful it was for you.

This one conversation does not have to lead to a full-blown witness right at that moment, but you are setting things up for an opportunity in the future.

Here is another example. As you are working with someone, an opportunity may come along that requires your organization to do something that is not completely ethical. What a great opportunity to begin a discussion with coworkers about the nature of ethics, and to brainstorm about possible ways around the dilemma. A statement of your Christian convictions in a nonjudgmental, matter-of-fact way is a great witness in and of itself, not to mention the opportunity it may provide for a more detailed witness later. On top of that, as the discussion progresses, you will have the opportunity to hear the beliefs of your co-workers about the nature of their moral principles.

These are just two possible examples of how you might get at the worldview questions. The first example above probed a little about question one, "What is the nature of ultimate reality?" The second example was getting at question number six, "How do we know what is right and wrong?"

You have to remember, though, it is not just about you asking them questions. In the course of a conversation, as you talk about a particular topic, they are learning about you and your beliefs as well. In this way, your witness has a chance to seep into their lives bit by bit over time. And as you interact and gather this understanding about them, there will come a time when it all comes together and you will be able to specifically talk about their salvation based on an understanding of where they are coming from.

ELICIT THEIR BELIEFS - ASK THE SEVEN WORLDVIEW QUESTIONS

Digging Deeper

1. Are you familiar and comfortable enough with the seven worldview questions that you would be able to use them as a tool to find out about the faith of another individual?

2. Which of the worldview questions will give you the most information about the faith foundation of an individual?

3. Besides giving you information that will better help you craft a witness, what other value can you receive by asking people these questions?

I am a fourth degree black belt in karate and have had many opportunities over the years to teach karate classes. Many of the classes I teach are for children. Some of them are rank beginners while others have been doing it a while and have already learned a few things.

It is this second group that tends to be the hardest to work with. Many of them think that what they have already learned makes them as knowledgeable as the teacher. There have been many occasions when I have tried to teach a young student something and the student tried to correct me. Imagine that! The student thinks he knows more than the teacher. When a person, for whatever reason, has no respect for the one they are interacting with, the end result is that the individual is not in a position to learn anything.

In our witnessing situations, we want the person we are addressing to be willing to listen to our witness. That will never happen unless we are able to develop an atmosphere where respect is granted.

Chapter 8
Create a Respectful Atmosphere

Periodically I make the effort to write a letter to the editor of our local newspaper related to some issue that is put in the public square. Whenever I do this, I only select topics that have some moral significance and which I feel strongly about.

Some time back there was some controversy in our local government commission when someone started making negative comments about the fact that the meeting was started off with prayer. You may recall that earlier in the book I mentioned having written a letter to the editor which brought about the conversation with Tom. It was actually my letter about prayer at the commission meeting that led to that interaction.

It is a pretty well known fact that the large majority of people don't have any problem with the practice of prayer before a public meeting. In recent times, however, a vocal minority has been able to impose their will on the majority in cases like this by claiming that there needs to be "separation of church and state."

I won't take the time to get into all of the reasons why this argument does not apply to this situation. Suffice it to say that my letter advocated for the point of view that having a prayer was not an endorsement of religion, and that it was a perfectly acceptable practice.

In our newspaper, whenever they print letters, they also

print the writer's e-mail address so that readers can contact the person directly if they wish. In this case I got four personal responses. One of them was simply to pat me on the back. The other three, however, completely disagreed with my position and proceeded to tell me why.

All three of these interactions led to back and forth conversations in which we responded to one other's objections. At first, all three of these people were quite strong in the way they attacked me and my position. But rather than answer in kind, I thanked them for responding and was careful to be kind and respectful to them in my reply.

The easy thing for me would have been just to blast back the way they tried to blast me. Had I done so, that probably would have pretty much ended the conversation. But I wanted to try and make this an opportunity to share my faith with them, so I responded in a way that allowed a dialogue to develop. In all three cases I was eventually able to share the gospel with them. One of those ended fairly quickly. With the other two, however, the conversation went on for several weeks and I had the opportunity to share my faith in significant detail, and even challenge their faith assumptions. It was an exciting opportunity.

I wish I could say that one of them accepted the Lord. That didn't happen with me. But I realize that I am not the whole witness. It is very possible that I have opened the door for someone else who will be able to lead them to know Christ. I do know one thing, though. If I hadn't made it a point to create an atmosphere for dialogue, I would never have had the opportunity to share the witness.

Significant relationships require legitimate communication – communication in which both parties are willing to listen to and respect what the other has to say. This does not mean you have to agree with the other person. But you do have to be willing to honestly listen to what they are saying. This also doesn't mean that you necessarily ever become "best buddies." But there is a tremendous opportunity for witness contained in every relationship if we will just create the atmosphere that allows it to take place.

Great relationships also require that you present an aura that is welcoming to other people. If others do not feel comfortable around you, they will not want to spend time with you.

Your Communication

Human beings have a built-in need to be understood. If they perceive that they are not being understood, they will not be able to move beyond that point. They will either keep forcing the point to try and make their partner understand, or simply quit trying to communicate.

I have read various accounts of American soldiers who became Prisoners of War (POWs) in Vietnam and were put in a prison that became known as the Hanoi Hilton. These prisoners were often housed by themselves in cells which were no more than six by seven feet. Being by themselves created tremendous isolation, but they developed a tapping code that allowed them to communicate with each other – which they did constantly. There are numerous stories of the prisoners concerning this very aspect of communication. It was the one thing that gave them strength to keep going in the midst of some very horrible circumstances.

The POW stories are an extreme case, but every human being has the same need, and will go to almost any lengths to be understood. You have a need to share what is on your heart and mind. But so does every other person.

One of the most powerful tools of relationship building involves your ability to allow your friend to feel understood. If you want another person to listen to you, you must also be willing to listen to them.

This is so powerful that the very best sales gurus include

listening as an integral part of their training programs. Listening can be used in such a way as to actually manipulate people. Of course, I am certainly not advocating manipulation. Manipulation ultimately will turn around to bite you. The point is, it is so powerful that it is recognized by professional persuaders as a tool that must not be overlooked.

One of the easiest ways to make this work for you is to simply ask your friend's opinion about something, then listen until they feel like you understand them. Be sure to get that last point. It is not enough that you actually understand them. They must *feel* that you do. Once that point is reached, then they will feel an obligation, even a compulsion, to hear your viewpoint.

Take the time to create genuine communication. It will facilitate relationship creation more than almost anything else you can do.

Your Aura

Another element related to developing a relationship which allows for an effective witness is to create an atmosphere where no one feels intimidated when talking to you about faith issues. Of course you believe that your faith in Jesus Christ is the truth and that other people's belief that Jesus Christ is not the way to salvation is not the truth. But you have to realize that they believe that their faith is true and that you are wrong.

The only way you will be able to present your case is if you have an attitude of respect toward the views of the other person. If you can do that, the opportunity to share why you believe they are wrong and you are right will, at some point, emerge. This doesn't mean that your friend will necessarily have a change of heart, but you will at least have the opportunity to present the evidence and allow them to make a decision.

When it comes to building new relationships, sometimes there is a down side to being a professional Christian minister

– not just for me, but for my wife, as well. Believe it or not, there are quite a few people out there who do not want to establish a relationship with a pastor or pastor's wife.

In years past, this was particularly frustrating for my wife, Deborah. She is a real "people person" and likes to make friends wherever she goes. When she realized that some people avoided her when they found out she was a pastor's wife, she decided that she would make it more difficult for them to do that.

Now don't get this wrong. She is really big on establishing friendships in order to create a witnessing opportunity, and she was not about to give that up. So she simply quit telling people that her husband was a pastor until after she had already made friends with them. Once they liked her, it was much harder for them to throw her out of their lives. Over the years, she has had great success doing this because she genuinely likes people and loves making new relationships. Her aura literally draws people to her.

If you want to be successful at developing relationships, you have to become a person that other people will like. If you do that, people will be drawn to you.

Ultimate Respect

The highest form of respect you can have toward another person is to love them no matter their beliefs. Certainly, use your relationships to share your faith. But don't let the fact that the other person does not immediately accept your faith affect whether or not the relationship continues to exist. You are not responsible for the decisions other people make. You are only responsible for doing the best you can to give them the opportunity to make a decision for themselves. You need to keep your relationships active. You never know when they will bear fruit.

There is never any need to put another person down

because of their beliefs. And there is never any reason to feel intimidated by anyone who might try to put you down. Every person has to ultimately make their own decision as it relates to Jesus Christ. Don't take another person's decision on your own shoulders. Witness to them and do your best to convince them. But ultimately the final decision is between the individual and God. Let it be that way. By showing respect, you will receive respect and the opportunity to present your witness.

Digging Deeper

1. Can you think of someone that you would have a difficult time witnessing to because there is some kind of tension between you and that person?

2. What weaknesses do you have in your listening skills that you should work on so that you can be a more effective witness? What can you do to improve your listening skills?

3. How easy do others find it to get close to you?

When I lived in Okinawa I got into scuba diving and really enjoyed that sport. Over a period of several years I also had opportunities to dive in other places such as Guam and Hawaii. But to me, Okinawa was the best.

There were several things that made Okinawa special. First, there were different places around the island which provided dramatically different diving experiences. There were also all kinds of beautiful coral and tropical fish. It was simply fantastic. Another special attraction was the fact that you didn't have to have a boat to get to the great diving spots. You could just swim out from shore.

As a part of my diving experience, I bought a camera and started doing some underwater photography. It is a little trickier doing it underwater than on the surface. For one thing, the camera was rather bulky and did not have all of the automatic features to control the focus and lighting like most surface cameras have. On top of that, many of the objects of my pictures were moving targets. The fish typically wouldn't stay still and pose for me. Getting a good shot was generally all about great preparation, with a lot of luck thrown in. You had to be ready when the opportunity presented itself or you missed your chance.

I actually got some very nice pictures. On the other hand, I also took a lot of really sorry ones. It all had to do with how well prepared I was when the opportunity arose.

Chapter 9
Be Ready When an Opportunity Presents Itself

One day I was having a conversation with another pastor and we began talking about the reasons why the Christian faith was the truth. It was kind of a strange conversation, though. It started out simply as a comment, but I have a particular interest in the topic so I delved deeper into it.

After just a short time, though, he completely changed the subject. It seemed a little strange, but I didn't think much about it at the time because our conversation was already wide ranging. However, that chat came to my mind later and I pondered why he had responded the way he did.

Then it hit me. He didn't want to talk about it because he himself felt uncomfortable talking to non-Christians from other belief systems. He was very good at simply sharing the gospel and had a tremendous track record of growing a church. His churches always had high baptismal numbers. But when it came to talking to people who didn't come from his worldview, he was clueless. Not that he wouldn't witness to them. He did! But if they did not already understand the God of the Bible, he simply didn't know how to bring them to that understanding.

It used to be that we could get away with that in America. But now there are just too many people with different worldviews. Sure there are still enough remaining from our own to allow us to specialize and feel good about all of the people that we are able to lead to the Lord. But that kind of specialization is going to leave more and more people without a witness.

And the biggest problem of all? It is getting more and more difficult to tell who these people might be. Many of the people who are first generation from some other culture might be obvious to us. We can recognize that the country they come from is primarily Islamic or Hindu or something else. But now, many home-grown Americans have gotten into other worldviews. Everywhere you look you will find people who are Atheists, New Agers, Wiccans, Muslims, and the list goes on. These are people who have been exposed to other worldviews right here in America and have deliberately chosen to follow them. This has been going on long enough that some of these home-grown folks are even second or third generation.

If we are going to take our Christian witness seriously, we have to be ready to share our faith in a way that makes sense to *them*. We can't simply decide to share our witness with some and not mess with the ones that are inconvenient for us.

We must be willing to prepare ourselves to share our faith with anyone we have the opportunity to interact with. This point should go without saying. But since so few are actually able do it, it must be overtly stated anyway. I think the reason so many people find this particular issue to be so difficult is because they are afraid that they are going to have to use it in situations where they feel uncomfortable.

What Is Wrong, Here?

What is it about sharing our faith that makes it so difficult? The importance of giving a witness is almost universally recognized by Christians to be an essential part of the faith. Many Christian denominations even have entire agencies dedicated to evangelism and missions. Why is it, then, that there is so much resistance? I believe there are several factors.

1. Christians don't care enough to learn what they need to know.

This is a hard indictment, but I don't think it is an unfair criticism. Now, certainly, there are those who do prepare themselves, and they are definitely to be commended. But the vast majority simply have never taken the time, or made the effort, to learn the basic information that a person needs to know to share their faith. There are all kinds of excuses that can be put forth, but I am not going to cut a lot of slack here. The fact is, the information is readily available for anyone who wants to learn it. When I first learned how to share my faith, it was from reading a book that taught how to do it. I simply got the book on my own and learned its method. These days there are books, websites, periodicals, classes and many other resources that are available to anyone who cares to learn.

2. Christians don't care enough to intentionally make relationships.

Perhaps this is another harsh accusation. But again, I don't think it is unfair. Once again, kudos to those who do it. But the percentage of Christians taking this step is relatively small. Christ's command is for us to take the initiative to go into the world and make disciples. We can't just sit around and wait for people to come up to us and beg for the information.

We are not going to make relationships with everyone we come into contact with. First it is impossible because of the sheer number of people. On top of that there are those who are simply not interested in allowing us into their lives. But that should not keep us from constantly probing. We can always be knocking on other people's doors and at the same time have our own door open to them. In that process, new relationships will develop. It is a sad thing when it is the Christian who is not interested and active in building new relationships.

3. The primary understanding of witness technique is a confrontational model.

Many Christians don't share their faith because a confrontational approach is very uncomfortable to them and they have never been taught, nor had modeled, any other way. To them, witnessing is simply scarey.

This image has been created because most witnessing methods have been designed in a way that assumes a confrontational situation. Virtually every witness training I have ever attended taught a method, then set up a time to go out and do cold call witnessing. The cold call situation does give practical experience and will produce some positive results. But it is extremely unnatural and uncomfortable for most people. As a result, many simply refuse to get the training.

I personally have done it, can do it, and will still do it in appropriate situations. But I must say, as an overall strategy I don't particularly care for that approach. That being said, it is no excuse for Christians to avoid learning how to present the gospel. If you are faithful to learn how to share your faith, there will come a time when it will be very natural and comfortable to tell someone what you believe. But if you have never taken the opportunity to learn how to do it, your witness will be greatly hampered.

4. Too many Christians do not feel spiritually qualified to share with other people.

Who is going to share Christ with another person when they, themselves, would feel like hypocrites if they did? And what non-Christian is going to listen to the witness of a person they consider a hypocrite?

The problem is, many Christians do not live a lifestyle

BE READY WHEN AN OPPORTUNITY PRESENTS ITSELF

that is consistent with the Christian faith. For instance, people who use profanity, have sexual affairs outside of marriage, abuse drugs and alcohol, go to movies and other activities that contain immoral material, view pornography, hold grudges, and the like, are going to be very uncomfortable telling a person that they need to get their lives aligned with a holy God. The Christian faith is not simply an intellectual pursuit. It is a life lived in relationship with God.

What You Can Do

You need to be ready, and thorough preparation is the way that happens. If you will become well equipped, you will find that it will do a couple of very important things for you. First, it will greatly bolster your confidence in your own faith. The gospel is the truth! And being able to articulate it means that you must organize the information concerning the gospel in a way that makes sense to you. The process of doing that creates great personal confidence. Secondly, it makes it possible for you to give a witness whenever there is an appropriate opportunity. You can't share what you have never taken the time to learn.

So let's look at the practical things you can do to prepare yourself to be ready to share your faith at any moment.

1. Know your own faith.

To know your own faith, you will have to study the Bible, understand your own worldview foundation and learn a gospel presentation. Frankly, this will take some effort on your part. But it is certainly not that difficult an undertaking.

You do, in fact, learn necessary information about virtually everything that you are really interested in. You have learned how to do your job (and every other job you have ever had), all the rules and skills for sports you enjoy, the things necessary to become proficient in hobbies you pursue, the likes and dislikes of family and friends – and the list could go on. If sharing your faith is important to you, you will learn how to do it. It is as simple as that.

2. *Know the faith of those you wish to witness to.*

Not only is it important to know your own faith, you need to know something about the faith of the person you want to share with. This does not mean that you have to become an expert in Christian apologetics and philosophy of religion. But it does mean that you will have to learn at least the basics of the other person's religion and understand their worldview. Again, this is not a difficult undertaking, but it will require that you spend some time and effort in order to pull it off. This is particularly important because you need this information in order to be sure that you are presenting the gospel in a way that makes sense to them from their theological background.

3. *Keep your personal relationship with God up to date.*

The first two points relate to what you need to know in order to share an effective witness. This one relates to who you must become. Christianity is not simply the intellectual acceptance of a set of propositions. If it was, it would be easy.

Certainly there is a set of beliefs that we have to know and understand. But the essence of the Christian faith is a personal relationship with a person. If our relationship with God is strained, it is going to be difficult, if not impossible, to bring ourselves to introduce other people to him. In that respect, it is not really different from what happens in human relationships.

If there are areas of your life which are out of tune with God, you must make the effort to repent and restore the fellowship. This may mean a change of attitude or a change of lifestyle. Whatever it means for you, it is a requirement for effective witness.

4. Cultivate relationships.

Once you have put yourself in a position to be able to give a witness, both intellectually and personally, you are ready to actually start letting God use your life. This means that you must begin to look around and find people you can start having relationships with. Not that everyone you meet will become your best friend. But it does mean that you must intentionally open yourself up and allow people to attach to your life. As you do this, the opportunities will naturally begin to emerge, and the witness that comes forth will be easy and natural.

Are You Ready?

I was watching a football game recently and with less than one minute left the score was tied. At that point, the team which had the ball had about ninety yards to go for a score. It looked for all the world like the game was about to go into overtime. In order to talk things over, the team with the ball called a time out.

After the time out, the team on offense ran from the sideline and directly to the line of scrimmage without going into a huddle. When they snapped the ball, the defensive team was caught completely off guard and were not yet in position. The confusion was so great, that the offense was able to get a great gain and nearly scored. And on the next play they did, and won the game – all because the other team was caught not being ready to play.

If we want to take our Christian faith seriously and be ready to play the game of life that God put us here for, we have to prepare ourselves in every way possible. An important part of that is to prepare ourselves for witness. We don't have to be overly aggressive and make ourselves repugnant to others, but we do have to be prepared.

Digging Deeper

1. Which of the four issues that hinder witness come closest to your situation? If it is none of those, is there some other reason that you are not as effective as you think you ought to be?

2. How well do you know the basics of your own faith?

3. How well do you know the basic tenets of the faith of non-Christians that you interact with?

Some time back, I was playing tennis with my son. As it happened, the tennis courts we were using were right beside a little league baseball diamond. While we were playing, there was a baseball practice going on, and once in a while I would look over and watch the young players taking batting practice.

One of the coaches was pitching and each of the boys took turns at the plate to practice their hitting. Some of the players were already very good and able to hit the ball quite effectively. There were others, though, who were not very good at all.

As I watched, I noticed something very interesting. It seems that the ones who were not very good were very timid at the plate. They did not stand with confidence, and their first reaction when the ball was thrown was to cringe and back off. The good ones, though, had an entirely different demeanor. When they saw the ball coming they literally attacked it. The results spoke for themselves.

What is true for hitting the baseball is true for other areas of life. We will find greater success with the things we attack with boldness.

Chapter 10
Speak with Boldness

By nature, I am not the kind of person that likes to get into arguments or heated discussions about my faith – or anything else for that matter. In fact, I don't even like watching those news shows where they bring in one person from the left and one from the right and let them argue out an issue for a few minutes before not coming to any kind of resolution.

That being said, when the situation demands it, I can operate in that kind of environment. In those situations, I do everything I can to create an atmosphere where the other person does not feel put down, but I am not hesitant about standing up for my faith.

A situation like that happened to me one day. I was sharing my views on the Christian faith, and a woman who disagreed with me jumped on the attack. Her attack, though, was not on the merits of what I had said. Rather, it was an emotional response because I was presenting a view that opposed her atheistic worldview.

During our brief conversation she made statements about how she didn't believe what I was saying, so I backed off a little and gave her a chance to tell me what she believed. Virtually everything she came out with had no firm foundation at all - either philosophical or scientific. It was basically an emotional appeal that expressed her opinion and her lifestyle desires.

When she had finished, I challenged her to back up her position. I asked her to explain to me why her point of view was valid. I asked her to explain what authority she was using to back up her position. At this, she babbled on a little bit and finally just left. I had not said anything mean or disrespectful to her, but I was bold in advocating my view.

Dealing with this issue may be one of the hardest things a Christian must grapple with. We want to give a good witness, yet at the same time not offend the person we are witnessing to. What we also have to realize is that the other person has something to say about it, too.

It is like fighting in a war or participating in a sport. We can develop the skills and a great game plan, but when we face the opponent, we recognize that they have done the same thing. They come with tactics and attitudes that don't necessarily give way to our plans. When we move forward, they oppose us and cause our plans to go awry. So, we have to evaluate our progress and change our strategy on the fly.

We don't have control over the response of the person we are witnessing to. If they are interested in what we have to say, or are at least cordial enough to listen, it is easy to give a coherent witness. But if they become militant and try to silence us, we have to respond in a more determined and focused way. Not that we must become militant ourselves, but stronger nonetheless. Some people will be respectful while others will hate your message so strongly that they will do all they can to destroy your ability to speak it.

Speaking with boldness does not mean to put someone else down or to out shout them. It just means standing firm with your beliefs in the face of opposition. This can be done while still displaying the utmost respect for the other person.

Primarily, boldness is a function of preparation. If you have not done the personal preparation that was spoken of above, you will not be in a position to speak with boldness.

SPEAK WITH BOLDNESS

Boldness requires confidence, and confidence requires that you know that you know the truth.

It also does not mean arrogance. It is absolutely possible to win the battle and lose the war. I have been on both sides of this situation. I have been in positions where I was able to outsmart and out debate another person, and when we parted company the person left and I never had the opportunity to share with them again. After that experience, the person was even more mad and less willing to listen to me, or anyone else, than they were before we talked. I have also had people do that to me. And basically it made me upset to the point where I didn't want anything to do with them again.

We have to always be careful to keep our purpose before us. That purpose is to present the gospel in a way that causes a person to personally consider opening their life to God. If you become confrontational and arrogant, they will feel more compelled to oppose you than to listen to you.

It is a skill to learn to speak with boldness while still displaying kindness and gentleness. That being said, it is important to be so confident in our personal faith that we cannot, ourselves, be swayed to another point of view. If we have that kind of foundation, we can then learn to discern specifically how we should express our faith in every situation. If we don't have that kind of certainty, we will be very weak and timid in our witness.

Boldness requires stepping out of your comfort zone based on a firm conviction that you have the truth. If you don't have that conviction, you will not be able to consistently express this principle.

Digging Deeper

1. Under what circumstances would you be willing to challenge someone who opposed your faith?

2. Under what circumstances would you not be willing to challenge someone who opposed your faith?

3. What can a person do to stand up for their faith in the face of opposition, yet do it in a way that does not offend others?

I deeply appreciate people who are committed to their beliefs. But it bugs me to death to watch people use their faith as a means of building themselves up. When I lived in Latvia I was involved in a church that was quite active. It was one of the larger churches in the city and even had a preaching point in a neighboring small town which didn't have the resources to support its own church. One of the lay leaders, in addition to his very active involvement in the home church, served as the pastor of this preaching point. By all accounts he was a very dedicated man.

However, I had occasion to work with him some and found out a little more of his "behind the scenes" demeanor. As it turns out, he was not quite the "saint" that he appeared to be on the surface. Not that he was immoral, or anything like that. Rather, he oozed a very false humility. While putting on a show of devotion, he was actually looking for ways to have other people look at his life and praise him for it. Rather than working to build up the Kingdom of God, he was really looking to build himself up.

Chapter 11
Don't Try to Win Points

I live in a college town where football is king. Florida State University has built a very powerful reputation as one of the elite football schools in the nation. There are several things that have gone into creating a winning record.

Of course, you have to start with the coach. Bobby Bowden, with his brilliant administrative and coaching ability, developed a plan and executed it to perfection. He took a team that for several years before he came had been about as low as one could be. On taking that team he worked to make the players believe in themselves. On top of that, he surrounded himself with other coaches who were some of the best in the world. And as he prepared to play other teams, he developed game plans that exploited the weaknesses of his opponents in order to defeat them.

But, obviously, it is not just about coaching. It is also about the players who actually get out on the field and play the game. One of Bobby's great strengths has been his ability to recruit well. Consistently, year after year, he has been able to come up with one of the top recruiting classes in the nation. He always gets a large number of the very best athletes.

But there is another element that goes into the mix. Football is a team sport. The athletes who ultimately make it to the very top of their profession understand that. But many very gifted athletes become so convinced of their own talent that they think they can do it all on their own. As a result, these players have such a cocky attitude that even their teammates don't like working with them. In a team sport, that is a problem.

Every once in a while, this kind of attitude gets to be such a problem that it actually affects the performance of the team. Thankfully it doesn't happen too often, but I have seen occasions where some of the most highly touted players in the nation have been kicked off the team because they just couldn't follow the rules or get along with teammates. It is better to use a player with a little less natural talent, than one who creates disunity on the team.

In football, as in any team sport, the ultimate outcome depends on everyone working together. It doesn't matter if you have a team full of superstars if the team loses every game. The point of putting on the pads and getting out on the field is to win games.

So just what is the point of sharing your faith? Is it to impress your church friends? Is it to gain personal prestige as a very "spiritual person?" Is it to set a record for baptisms? Unfortunately, for some people, witnessing is viewed more as a competition. Getting someone to accept Christ somehow puts a feather in their cap. When a person has this kind of an attitude, sharing Christ becomes all about them.

Back in my seminary days, I was friends with a person who was on the staff of a large church. One day we were having a conversation about his church work and he made the comment that he had a quota for bringing a certain number of new people into the church every month. As we talked further, he revealed that every staff member was given a quota, and if they didn't meet it there were severe penalties. Now, I understand the need to grow the church, bring in new people and fund the programs. But a quota for witnessing? That was a little too much for me.

There are two things that need to be understood here. First

DON'T TRY TO WIN POINTS

and foremost, witnessing is all about God, not about us. The point is not for us to set records. It is for individuals to come into a personal relationship with God through Jesus Christ.

Secondly, *we* don't win people to Christ. When a person opens their life to God, it is God who has made it happen. God will use our witness as the vehicle for getting the message out, but our witness does not save people. The act of accepting Christ is something that is strictly between an individual and God. And the change that happens when a person does that is a work of God in the heart of the individual. We have nothing to do with the final outcome. We are simply the messengers.

Having pride in how effective we are as witnesses demonstrates the utmost in arrogance. What we need to focus on is developing relationships that allow us to share the message. We are called simply to speak the truth in love. After that, it is between the individual and God.

Can God use us even if our attitude is wrong? Of course he can! But that doesn't change the fact that we have nothing to do with the change. It also doesn't help our case before God. He is not impressed by our numbers. What impresses him is our willingness to serve him with the right attitude.

Digging Deeper

1. What is the meaning of the statement, "Witnessing is about God, not about us?"

2. What place do numbers and record keeping have in a witnessing context?

3. What causes Christians to begin to think that the ultimate result of a witnessing encounter depends on how well they do their presentation?

When I lived in Japan, I had a Japanese teacher who was a very committed Christian and a genuinely wonderful person. His testimony about how he came to Christ was very unusual, however. He shared with me that he prayed to receive Christ into his life the very first time he ever heard the gospel presented to him.

When he shared that, he went on to tell us that of those Japanese people who ultimately come to know Christ, the average amount of time it takes is about two years from the first time they hear a witness. He went on to explain that it generally takes fully a year for someone to simply understand the concept that there is only one God, then another year to ponder it and come to a decision.

When it comes to making such a radical change in one's life as to convert to a different worldview, it is important to realize that for most people it simply takes time to process the new way of thinking. As such, we have to be willing to invest our lives into another person for an extended period of time, rather than simply blowing them off if they do not receive Christ the first time we share with them.

Chapter 12
Think Long Term

I have been a student of personal change for quite a number of years, and a lot of what I have studied has been myself – my own efforts at personal change. In fact, I sometimes speak to businesses and associations on that very topic, and have even written books on personal development and the change process.

On a personal level, there have been so many times in my life when I wanted to make some kind of change and I found that it was just plain hard. There have, of course, been a few times when a dramatic change happened almost instantaneously, but those times have been rather rare. That kind of change was usually the result of some very dramatic or emotional event that suddenly and unexpectedly happened.

But most of the change I have tried to create in my life has been hard fought. There have been times when I wanted to become physically conditioned or to lose weight or to get rid of a bad habit. These kinds of things almost never happen quickly and easily. Why do you suppose that is the case? Let's look at one example, for a moment, and see if we can pick up on the reasons for the difficulty.

Almost everyone I have ever met has had some time in their life when they wanted to get physically conditioned. Yet you look around and the number of people who are actively working on it at any given time is relatively small. Even worse, those who stay with it for a period of years (as a lifestyle) are even fewer than that. Why is it that everyone wants it but so few actually pull it off? There are a number of factors that go into the difficulty, but let's look at the major reasons.

The first reason why many people have difficulty is that they have never clearly identified their goals. There is an old expression that says, "If you are not aiming at anything, you are sure to hit it." This is certainly true when trying to become physically conditioned. You must have some understanding of what you are trying to accomplish or you will never know when you have achieved success.

A second reason is that many people simply don't know the specific steps they need to take in order to reach their goals. It is easy, in general, to figure out what you need to do to get physically conditioned. You must work on weight control, you need some kind of cardiovascular element, and you need a muscle flexibility and strengthening component.

But each of these things requires a certain specific knowledge in order to be effective. You have to be careful that you don't work your muscles in ways that cause damage. You have to be sure that your aerobic conditioning program is geared to your personal situation. You have to learn what kinds of foods you need to eat and in what quantities. Unfortunately, many people are not willing to make the effort that is necessary to gain this knowledge. And without it, their efforts at conditioning will not be very efficient.

There is a third reason, and this one is typically very difficult to work though. Our bodies actually have a physiological bias against change. At any given time in your life, you have a default set of habits that support the physical conditioning you currently have. Your body is used to processing certain kinds of foods, your muscles are used to a particular level of exertion and your cardiovascular system is habituated to a particular level of work. You are currently the way you are now because you have created a set of life habits that have put you there. A change in any one of those areas requires an extra exertion of energy over an extended period of time. When you factor in that you have to create change in all of the areas at the same time, you can see the complexity of the problem and the high level of difficulty.

It is not too difficult to maintain a new conditioning plan for a week or two. But to actually change our physiology, we have to keep it up for at least several months. After a couple of weeks our bodies simply begin to rebel. We begin having cravings for bad foods, we start looking for excuses to miss a day of our workout routine, we become fatigued, and so on.

The fourth, and final, reason for the difficulty is spiritual. We have, over time, become very comfortable with how we are. And though we don't necessarily like some of the side effects of that condition, the condition itself is cozy. The food we eat makes us feel good, and not exerting our muscles and cardiovascular system is a comfortable default. The bottom line is, at a certain level we want to change, but at the very deepest level, we don't.

If we truly want to generate change in our physical conditioning, we have to create an inner drive, and an effective system, that is stronger than the internal resistance we are bound to come up against.

Now then, let's take this principle and think about how it affects our witnessing situation. Consider, for a moment, the people you want to witness to. What is going on in their lives? If we can understand that, it makes it a little easier to have patience with them as they process our gospel presentation.

We tend to think that sharing the gospel is simply an intellectual exercise. We share the knowledge, then the person we are sharing with simply believes it and become a Christian. Certainly that is one element of the process. But that would be like saying that getting physically conditioned is simply an intellectual exercise. There is the mental component that must be dealt with, but there is so much more.

When a person invites Christ into their life, a change takes place that requires their whole life to be reoriented. And the fact is, they have a habitual lifestyle that they have already become comfortable with. That doesn't mean that they necessarily like it, but they have learned to live with it, and changing will require major work.

Just exactly what will they have to change? They may have to change their friends, what they do with their time, the activities they participate in, the substances they put into their bodies, the way they talk, the way they think about life, and perhaps even their occupation. Wow, that is some really dramatic stuff. And it is not just that they have to follow a new list of do's and don'ts. They actually have to reorient their entire lifestyle and way of thinking.

It would be hard enough if this was like becoming physically conditioned and simply required the person to develop a system for change and follow it faithfully. But when a person is dealing with making a commitment to Christ, there is also an element of spiritual warfare that comes into play. Satan does not want to lose one of his own, and will put enormous pressure on a person's very spirit to keep him or her from going to the other side. So is it any surprise that it may take a person some time to process all of this and decide whether or not they want to do it?

For most people, it simply takes time for them to completely understand the message of the gospel and its implications for their life. It is simply not very easy to come to a place in one's life where there is a willingness to embrace the life change that is required when one accepts Christ. We need to create an atmosphere where the gospel can incubate in people's consciousness. This means making friendships and sticking with the relationships for the long term.

When the opportunity appears for you to tell someone what you believe, you really don't know where they are in their processing. Your opportunity may be the first time they have ever heard anything like that, and they are just trying to understand the meaning of what you are saying. Or maybe you are the third person they have heard and some things are just beginning to make sense. Or maybe your word is the twentieth time and they really are ready to make a decision. You have to discern that. If you try to force them to make a decision before they can really understand what you are talking about, you are not doing them, or God, any favors. You are trying to press an advantage using your own power.

Don't necessarily try to bring people to faith the first time you talk to them. There are times to do that, but that will be the exception rather than the rule for most people. If you are consistent, the right opportunity will eventually come. If you try to close the deal before they are ready and they reject Christ, the door may be closed to you forever. Always leave the door open for another opportunity.

Digging Deeper

1. Which of the issues related to change do you think are the most difficult for most people to deal with? Why?

2. Why do you think that it takes many people some length of time to understand the implications of the gospel message to the point where they become willing to accept it?

3. Why should a Christian not become discouraged when a person does not immediately accept Christ when a witness is given?

I'll admit that there are certain people that I don't particularly care to be around. I think we can all identify with that sentiment to some extent. Certainly some of those people are just bad folks, but not all of them.

There are cases when whether or not to spend time with a particular individual is strictly my own choice. But in other cases, I really don't have much of a choice. Life circumstances have simply put me in proximity to them. There are still others that, for some reason, have taken a liking to me and want to be around me. With this group, I have another choice to make – do I want to simply ignore them or give them the benefit of whatever it is that they find helpful in me?

I want to be the kind of person who helps people any way I can. I recognize that God's purpose for my life is not just about me. He wants to use my life to reach into the lives of others who need him. Sometimes this means developing relationships with people who might not, under normal circumstances, be my first choice.

Chapter 13
Relationship Road

A number of years ago I worked under a man named Joe (not his real name). Joe was brought from the outside and inserted as a supervisor over my area after I had been working with my organization for quite a number of years. Overall he was a good person, but he had a bit of a chip on his shoulder.

One of the things he wanted to do right off the bat was to assert his authority and let everyone know he was the boss. After a time, he called me into his office and we began to discuss an equipment request I had submitted. Apparently he had misinterpreted my justification for needing the equipment and began to attack me for subverting his authority.

At that point, I was completely caught off guard. I had no idea this was coming. In fact, even though he had been on the job several months, this was the first time I had actually met him in person.

After we talked a little more and he had a chance to hear my explanation, it became obvious to him that he had misinterpreted what I had requested – and to his credit he backed off. But he never did apologize for attacking me like he did. And from that day forward I had a low opinion of him. Over a several year period, I had numerous other occasions to interact with him, but that first encounter set the stage for the entire future of our relationship. He was my supervisor so I had to act civil toward him, but we never became friends. And I would do what I had to do as I interacted with him on the job, but after that I never had any enthusiasm about working with him.

You will not become best friends with everyone you meet. In fact, statistics show that the average person will only have a small handful of ultra close friends in an entire lifetime. But you do have the opportunity throughout your life to create scores of friendships that help make life meaningful. You have the chance, in the course of your life, to create a level of relationship that allows you the opportunity to share your faith.

The key to effective witness is not our proficiency in crafting and delivering a well thought out gospel presentation. This is not meant to minimize the role we play in presenting the gospel message. But, it is God's active work in people's lives that actually creates the change. For some reason, God has chosen to use human beings as instruments in that process. But our part has nothing to do with any actual change that takes place. We are only the messengers.

Every individual was created with a free will. God's plan for us is to use our lives to love other people in a way that creates free and open relationships that allow for a witness. In order for that to happen, we have to personally decide to enter relationships when opportunities open up. It is up to each individual to respond to God. As a witness, our part is simply to provide them with the information they need to make a decision.

The other part of the equation is what God does. When people invite Christ into their lives, God performs a miracle and makes them a new creature. He attaches himself to their life in a way that did not exist before. As a witness, we have nothing to do with that. Our part in the process is as a messenger. We are simply the storehouse of knowledge that people need in order make the decision. We can encourage and we can provide information. That is about it.

But in order to effectively do that, we need to build relationships that make us available to people when they need what we have. Our part may not be dramatic. And it may not be glamorous. But it is the part God has given us. It is up to us to become as effective as possible to facilitate this process.

Consider Mutee'a Al-Fadi. He was a Muslim who grew up in Saudi Arabia. He grew up hating Christians and believing that God wanted all Christians destroyed.

When he finished high school, he had the opportunity to go to college in a Western country. He was afraid, though, because he believed that he was going into the heart of an evil place. After about a month, he was feeling a bit lonely and heard about a program that teamed international students up with families in the community, and he decided to sign up in order to learn a little more about the local culture. The family that "adopted" him was very nice and treated him quite kindly over a period of about seven months. During that time, they never did anything that would cause him to feel uncomfortable related to religion. He really did enjoy the atmosphere of their family, but it didn't even dawn on him that they might be Christians.

One day they invited him to their house, and before the meal they asked a blessing. This shocked him and he was a bit dismayed. But the love they had shown him was exceedingly stronger than anything he had ever experienced among his Muslim friends and family. This really got him thinking and questioning what he had been taught. From that experience he decided to begin researching Christianity.

Several years later, after college, he was working with a company and met another person who was a faithful follower of Christ. This man really took an interest in him and made the effort to reach out and become a friend. As Mutee'a met this man's family, he was really impressed and it reminded him of the family who had treated him so nicely during college. Over time, he heard his new friend's testimony about how he had come to Christ.

More impressed than ever about a God who was able to change people's lives, Mutee'a began to attend a church, and within a year had given his life to Christ.

Let me tell you about one more person; a personal friend of mine whose life has been dramatically changed by his relationship with Christ. I have heard Heeth Varnedoe share his testimony with me personally, but now anyone can read about it in his wonderful autobiography, *Called to Excellence*, published by Evergreen Press.

Heeth started working for Flowers Baking Company in Thomasville, GA when he was a teenager, just doing odd jobs. But being a bright guy and a quick study, he caught the attention of the higher ups and they encouraged him. By the time he finished his degree at the University of Georgia, he was working at Flowers full time. He started at the bottom, but gradually worked his way up the company ladder to finally become the CEO. Under his leadership the company made the Fortune 500 list. By all accounts he had it made; beautiful family, lots of money, prestige, and a powerful position. Everyone would call him a huge success. But he was not a happy man. Inside he felt empty and his family was falling apart.

One day his wife, Jacqueline, got involved with some friends who led her to the Lord. Heeth liked the change he saw, but was not too interested in having Christ change his own life that way. In fact, at one point he told Jacqueline that he didn't want to hear the word "Jesus" in his house again.

But as his personal dissatisfaction with life became stronger, he began to interact with some Christians, himself. About that time he was befriended by a Christian businessman whose daily life demonstrated what the Christian life was all about. Some time after that, he had another opportunity to meet a pastor who helped him to see that he really needed God. But he still resisted until one day he realized that it was either God or a totally miserable life.

When he finally chose God, his life changed. And it was evident, not only in his personal satisfaction about life, but in the way he felt about his family and the way he treated the people in the company.

But none of this would have happened had not there been people who cared about his spiritual life and invested into him by their relationships. These were people who understood where he was coming from and were able to share with him on his level.

And this is what worldview witnessing is all about. It concerns caring enough about people to learn where they are in their relationship with God, then figuring out what you need to do to share a witness that they will understand. It is about being willing to put yourself out a little bit in order to make a deliberate effort to craft a gospel presentation that will communicate the love of God, in a way that is understandable to those who need to hear it.

There is nothing magic about it. It is simply a matter of understanding the responsibility that God has given us, and being willing to learn the things necessary to give a good witness. Then we must take that knowledge and apply it to the relationships we make in our lives. God cares for every person. He wants to use us to touch those who do not know him. When we do, God will work in their lives. And many of them will make the choice to follow him.

Digging Deeper

1. How many people in your life gave you a witness that ultimately led to you receiving Christ (and who were they)?

2. How long did it take from the first time you heard a gospel witness until you finally accepted Christ?

3. What were the most important factors related to why you finally decided to enter into a personal relationship with Jesus Christ?

Author Biographical Information

Dr. Freddy Davis is involved in a wide variety of ministry activities. He is an, author, seminar speaker, Executive Director of MarketFaith Ministries, pastor and the owner of TSM Enterprises.

Freddy received his BS in Communications from Florida State University as well as an MDiv and DMin from Southwestern Baptist Theological Seminary. He spent more than 6 years overseas serving as a missionary (11 years in Japan and 5 years in the former Soviet Republic of Latvia).

Churches and other Christian organizations which would like to have Freddy speak on the practical implications of worldview, particularly as it relates to living the Christian life and sharing an effective witness, may contact him through the MarketFaith Ministries website at www.marketfaith.org.

Freddy also speaks to businesses and other organizations on the topics of personal development, decision making, influence, customer service and leadership.

He lives in Tallahassee, Florida with his wife, Deborah.

For more information...

To inquire about speaking engagements or about obtaining other worldview resources, contact Freddy by e-mail at info@marketfaith.org.

Or you may fax him at 850-514-4571.

You may also visit the MarketFaith Ministries website at http://www.marketfaith.org.

Printed in the United States
200431BV00001B/13-165/A